SCARCITY MINDSET HIDDEN BRAIN

UNVEILING THE SUBCONSCIOUS FORCES THAT SHAPE OUR CHOICES

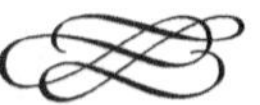

MARK R. WILLIAM

Copyright © 2024 by Mark R. William

All rights reserved.

No part of this book may be reproduced in any form or by any electronic or mechanical means, including information storage and retrieval systems, without written permission from the author, except for the use of brief quotations in a book review.

CONTENTS

INTRODUCTION

What is the "Scarcity Mindset"?

In the bustling intersections of our daily lives, amidst the myriad decisions we constantly face, lurks an invisible force that subtly yet powerfully shapes our choices: the scarcity mindset.

At its core, the scarcity mindset is a deep-seated belief that there isn't enough—be it time, resources, love, or opportunity. This perspective can pervade every aspect of our lives, often manifesting in feelings of fear, stress, and anxiety. When entrenched in this mindset, we often find ourselves consumed by the idea of lacking, which can blind us to the opportunities and abundance that surround us.

The Role of the "Hidden Brain" in Shaping Our Perceptions and Behaviors

Enter the "hidden brain"—a term that encapsulates the intricate web of unconscious processes, biases, and heuristics that silently guide our behavior. While our conscious brain is busy planning, reasoning, and making intentional decisions, the hidden brain operates behind the scenes, drawing from a vast reservoir of past experiences, cultural norms, and deeply ingrained evolutionary instincts.

The hidden brain plays a pivotal role in the proliferation of the scarcity mindset. Without our awareness, it filters and interprets the vast array of information we receive every second, often accentuating potential threats or losses. In a world brimming with stimuli, our hidden brain frequently resorts to shortcuts, amplifying signals of scarcity even when they may not accurately represent reality.

Understanding the interplay between the scarcity mindset and the hidden brain is crucial. Awareness is the first step towards change. By recognizing the subconscious forces at play, we can begin to challenge and reshape our deeply rooted beliefs and perceptions, opening the door to a life lived not in the shadow of what we lack, but in the light of the endless possibilities that lie ahead.

THE EVOLUTIONARY ROOTS OF SCARCITY

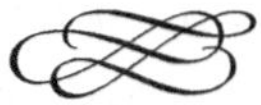

HOW OUR ANCESTORS' NEED FOR SURVIVAL INFLUENCES MODERN BEHAVIORS

In the lush, untamed landscapes of our prehistoric world, our ancestors lived a life markedly different from our modern existence. Their primary concern was not mortgage payments, work deadlines, or social media updates. Instead, it was a primal and ever-present focus: survival. To understand the underpinnings of our modern scarcity mindset, we must first journey back to these ancient times, where the seeds of our brain's evolutionary programming were sown.

HOW OUR ANCESTORS' NEED FOR SURVIVAL INFLUENCES MODERN BEHAVIORS

Life for early humans was punctuated by uncertainties. Food was not a guarantee but something that had to be hunted or foraged, often at great personal risk. Shelter was makeshift, at the mercy of the elements. And the threat of predators lurked at every corner. In this unpredictable environment, the human brain began to evolve specific mechanisms to ensure survival.

One of these mechanisms was an acute sensitivity to scarcity. When resources were limited, early humans had to be adept at recognizing and responding to signs of potential shortage. If a particular fruit-bearing tree bore fewer fruits one season, it signaled a possible food crisis in the future. Recognizing such signs early on could mean the difference between life and death.

As a result, those with brains attuned to detecting and avoiding scarcity were more likely to survive and pass on their genes. Over generations, this heightened sensitivity to scarcity became embedded in our DNA, giving rise to behaviors that prioritize immediate needs and potential threats over long-term planning or abstract thinking.

In today's world, while we're not typically faced with life-or-death situations on a daily basis, these ancient neural pathways remain active. The scarcity mindset of our ancestors manifests in modern anxieties about money, job security, and social status. We stockpile resources, often beyond our actual needs, driven by an unconscious fear rooted in our evolutionary history.

THE BRAIN'S DEFAULT MODE: FIGHT OR FLIGHT

Central to our ancestors' survival toolkit was the brain's "fight or flight" response—a rapid, automatic reaction to perceived threats. When confronted with a danger, such as a looming predator, the body would release a surge of adrenaline, preparing the individual to either confront the threat (fight) or flee to safety (flight).

While this response was crucial for our ancestors, it can be maladaptive in our contemporary society. When we perceive threats in our modern lives, whether it's a looming work deadline or a confrontational colleague, our body often reacts as if we're facing a life-threatening predator. Our heart rate increases, our muscles tense up, and our focus narrows.

This ancient system, designed for immediate physical threats, is frequently activated in response to modern psychological stresses, which can exacerbate feelings of scarcity and deficit. For example, when faced with financial strain, our fight or flight response might kick in, leading to panic, rash decisions, or avoidance—none of which are productive in addressing the actual challenge.

The evolutionary roots of scarcity run deep. They have been shaped and honed by countless generations of survival and adaptation. By understanding where these instincts come from and recognizing when they're at play in our modern lives, we can better navigate the challenges of today, armed with the wisdom of our past. In the next chapters, we will delve into strategies for recognizing and managing these ancient responses in a world where they often represent more of an obstacle than a help.

THE PSYCHOLOGY OF SCARCITY

HOW SCARCITY AFFECTS OUR DECISION-MAKING PROCESSES

Diving deeper into the complexities of the human mind, it becomes evident that scarcity plays a paramount role in shaping our thoughts, behaviors, and decisions. Beyond our evolutionary instincts, the scarcity principle has found its way into our daily interactions and the very fabric of our society. From the lines that form outside a store during a limited-time sale to the way we value rare collectibles, the influence of scarcity is omnipresent.

At its core, scarcity generates a sense of urgency. When we believe something is in short supply, our brain shifts into a mode of heightened alertness. This often leads to what psychologists term the "scarcity tunnel vision," where our focus narrows down to the scarce resource, often at the expense of other, equally important factors.

For example, someone on a tight budget may become so preoccupied with finding discounted items that they overlook the overall quality or long-term value of a purchase. Similarly, in a professional setting, the fear of missing out on a scarce opportunity might push individuals to make hasty decisions without thoroughly evaluating all potential implications.

- **Cognitive Biases and Scarcity:** This narrowed perspective can lead to cognitive biases. One such bias is the "loss aversion" principle. Humans, by nature, tend to feel the pain of losing something twice as intensely as the pleasure of gaining something of equivalent value. In situations of scarcity, the fear of loss becomes magnified, pushing individuals to make decisions that prioritize short-term gains or the avoidance of immediate losses, even if it means sacrificing long-term benefits.
- **The Urgency of Now:** Scarcity introduces a sense of immediacy. When something is in short supply, whether it's time, money, or another resource, the need to act swiftly often takes precedence. This can lead to impulsive decisions without proper reflection or evaluation. The "limited-time offers" in retail or the "last piece left" tactic are classic examples of how businesses harness this urgency to drive consumer action.
- **Cognitive Bandwidth and Overload:** Research suggests that scarcity consumes our cognitive resources, leaving less "mental bandwidth" for other tasks. This is especially true when the scarcity is related to fundamental needs, such as food or shelter. When preoccupied with pressing concerns, our cognitive capacity to process information, solve problems, and make informed decisions can diminish, leading to potential errors or oversights.
- **Decision Fatigue and Scarcity:** Repeatedly facing scarcity-induced decisions can lead to what's known as "decision fatigue." As we make more decisions in a state of scarcity, our ability to make good choices can deteriorate. Over time, this can lead to a reliance on default choices or avoidance of decisions altogether.

- **Emotional Responses and Their Impact:** Scarcity often evokes strong emotional reactions, such as stress, anxiety, or fear. These emotions can cloud judgment, leading to reactive rather than proactive decisions. For instance, the fear of missing out (FOMO) can push individuals to commit to opportunities without thorough evaluation, driven by the emotional dread of potential regret.

THE RELATIONSHIP BETWEEN SCARCITY AND VALUE PERCEPTION

One of the most intriguing aspects of scarcity is how it alters our perception of value. A principle well-understood and often exploited in marketing and economics, the notion is straightforward: the rarer an item or opportunity, the more valuable it appears.

Consider collectibles or limited-edition items. Their inherent value isn't necessarily tied to their functionality or utility but to their rarity. The belief that "fewer" means "more valuable" is a psychological construct rooted in our scarcity-driven mindset.

This perception extends beyond physical goods. Opportunities, experiences, and even relationships can be perceived as more valuable when they're deemed scarce. Events labeled as "once in a lifetime" or relationships where someone's time and attention are seen as limited can intensify our desire to pursue and cherish them.

However, there's a caveat. While scarcity can enhance value perception, it can also lead to irrational behaviors or decisions. The allure of a scarce resource might blind us to its actual worth, causing overvaluation. This overvaluation can lead to regret when the true value of the resource becomes apparent outside the blinding scope of scarcity.

The intricate dance between scarcity and our psychological processes is complex and deeply rooted in our evolutionary history. By understanding these patterns, we can begin to make more informed decisions, reducing the influence of scarcity on our lives. The next chapters will explore real-life examples and strategies to manage and counteract the effects of a scarcity-driven mindset.

THE HIDDEN BRAIN AT WORK

As we navigate through life, we often like to believe that our decisions are entirely rational, based on clear thought processes and analysis. However, beneath our conscious reasoning lies a powerful entity called the "hidden brain." This subconscious force can often push us in directions based on past experiences, societal inputs, and even primitive survival instincts. The scarcity mindset is one such perspective deeply embedded by our hidden brain, affecting various aspects of our daily lives.

Shopping Habits and the Influence of the Hidden Brain

The act of shopping, whether for necessities, luxury items, or even experiences, is deeply intertwined with the hidden brain's workings. Many of our buying choices are not based solely on logical reasoning, but are instead influenced by subconscious cues, past experiences, societal norms, and, most importantly, our perception of scarcity.

- **Fear of Missing Out (FOMO)**: One of the most powerful tools marketers use to tap into the hidden brain is the induction of FOMO. By creating an illusion of scarcity —"only 2 items left in stock!" or "sale ends in 2 hours!"— merchants encourage customers to make quick decisions. The subconscious fear of missing a good deal or a desired item pushes the hidden brain into action, often leading to impulse buying.
- **Brand Loyalty and Past Experiences**: Our hidden brain remembers past experiences, both positive and negative. If someone had a great experience with a particular brand, the subconscious might favor that brand in future purchases without an in-depth analysis of other options. Similarly, a past negative experience with a brand can subconsciously steer a consumer away, even if the brand has improved its offerings.
- **Social Conformity and Trends**: The desire to fit in or be part of a group is deeply rooted in our psyche. The hidden brain often prompts us to purchase items or experiences that are perceived as "trendy" or popular among our peers. This is why viral trends, whether in fashion, tech, or lifestyle, see a surge in sales. The underlying subconscious message here is the fear of being left out or appearing 'outdated.'
- **Emotional Purchases**: Emotions play a significant role in shopping habits. People often buy items to celebrate, to cope with stress or sadness, or even out of boredom. The hidden brain associates shopping with a feel-good factor or relief, pushing individuals to shop even when it might not be financially prudent.
- **Anchoring Effect**: The first price we see for a product often becomes the anchor against which we judge the value of subsequent products. For instance, if the first shirt we see in a store is priced at $100, and the next one is $50, our hidden brain perceives the second shirt as a bargain, even if it

might still be overpriced. Retailers often use this psychological trick, placing higher-priced items at the entrance, making other products seem cheaper in comparison.

- **Post-purchase Rationalization**: After making a purchase, especially an impulsive one, our hidden brain seeks to justify the decision. We tend to focus on the positive aspects of the item and downplay any negatives. This mental gymnastics is a protective mechanism to avoid feelings of buyer's remorse.

INTERPERSONAL RELATIONSHIPS AND THE INTRICACIES OF THE HIDDEN BRAIN

Interpersonal relationships, be it familial, romantic, platonic, or professional, form the crux of human experience. These connections shape our lives in profound ways. However, beneath the surface of our conscious actions and reactions in relationships lies the intricate web of the hidden brain. Its silent nudges, formed from past experiences, cultural norms, and ingrained beliefs, heavily influence our interactions and perceptions.

- **Attachment Styles**: Born from early life experiences, particularly with primary caregivers, our attachment styles play a pivotal role in how we relate to others. The hidden brain remembers feelings of security or abandonment from childhood, influencing whether we become anxiously attached, avoidantly attached, or securely attached in our adult relationships.
- **Scarcity Mindset in Love**: A person who believes that love is scarce might cling to relationships, even toxic ones, out of fear of being alone. This mindset can also manifest as jealousy or the fear that there isn't enough love to go around, driving possessive behaviors.

- **Past Traumas and Defense Mechanisms**: Past traumas, betrayals, or heartbreaks leave imprints on our hidden brain. Without conscious awareness, individuals might project past insecurities onto current relationships, expecting history to repeat itself. This can lead to unjust suspicions, lack of trust, or overprotectiveness.
- **Social Comparison**: Our hidden brain often engages in social comparisons, evaluating our relationships against others'. This might result in feelings of inadequacy or superiority, affecting the natural flow of interactions. The societal narrative of what relationships 'should' look like can deeply influence our satisfaction levels.
- **Seeking Validation**: The subconscious desire for validation can shape interactions. Some might constantly seek approval, driven by a deep-seated belief of not being 'enough'. This can lead to people-pleasing behaviors, suppressing one's needs, or avoiding confrontations.
- **Communication Patterns**: Our hidden brain dictates our communication patterns based on early life observations. If a child observes parents avoiding conflicts, they might grow up avoiding tough conversations. Conversely, if raised in a volatile environment, the hidden brain might prompt aggressive or defensive communication.
- **Love Languages**: While Dr. Gary Chapman's concept of the five love languages is a conscious understanding, our preference for a particular love language might stem from subconscious experiences. For instance, if gifts were used as a means of apology in childhood, an individual might subconsciously equate gifts with love in adulthood.
- **Boundary Setting**: Our ability or inability to set boundaries is often a reflection of our subconscious beliefs about self-worth. Those with a deeply ingrained belief of not being worthy might struggle to set boundaries, fearing rejection or conflict.

WORK ENVIRONMENT AND THE UNDERPINNINGS OF THE HIDDEN BRAIN

The modern workspace, whether it's a bustling office, a digital platform, or a serene home setting, is not just about tasks and objectives. It's a dynamic mesh of interactions, aspirations, pressures, and cultures. Beneath the observable behaviors and decisions in a work environment, the hidden brain is constantly at play, guiding actions and reactions based on ingrained beliefs, past experiences, and societal constructs.

- **Perception of Value and Self-worth**: Based on past experiences or societal norms, our hidden brain often dictates our perceived value in the workplace. An employee who subconsciously believes they're not "good enough" may hesitate to ask for raises, promotions, or even voice opinions during meetings.
- **Competition and Scarcity Mindset**: In workplaces that emphasize limited resources, be it promotions, bonuses, or recognitions, the hidden brain can drive an unhealthy competitive spirit. Employees might hoard information, undermine colleagues, or engage in office politics, all driven by the fear of missing out.
- **Response to Feedback**: Our hidden brain interprets feedback based on past experiences. An individual who faced criticism in early life might become defensive or overly self-critical when receiving feedback, viewing it as a personal attack rather than constructive criticism.
- **Adaptability to Change**: Resistance or adaptability to change often stems from the subconscious. An individual who equates change with instability, based on past experiences, might resist new systems or tools, even if they're beneficial.
- **Communication Styles**: The hidden brain plays a pivotal role in how one communicates. If someone grew up in an

environment where open communication was discouraged, they might avoid direct confrontations or withhold opinions in professional settings.

- **Work-Life Balance**: Our subconscious beliefs about success and dedication can influence work-life balance. If an individual subconsciously equates long hours with dedication and success, they might overwork and neglect personal well-being.
- **Team Dynamics and Groupthink**: The hidden brain's desire for social acceptance and fear of isolation can lead to groupthink, where employees agree with a decision for the sake of harmony, even if they believe it's not the best choice.
- **Leadership Styles**: Leadership is heavily influenced by subconscious beliefs. A leader who grew up in a strict hierarchical setting might adopt an autocratic style, while one who values collaboration might lean towards a democratic approach.
- **Approach to Failure**: Our hidden brain's association with failure, based on past experiences, can determine how we respond to setbacks. Some might view failures as learning opportunities, while others might see them as personal shortcomings, leading to self-doubt or avoidance of challenging tasks.
- **Innovation and Risk-taking**: The willingness to innovate or take risks is also tied to our subconscious. If an individual has faced repercussions for mistakes in the past, their hidden brain might caution against trying new methods or venturing into uncharted territories.

REAL-LIFE EXAMPLES OF THE HIDDEN BRAIN PERPETUATING A SCARCITY MINDSET

The Toilet Paper Scare: A Deep Dive into the Phenomenon
with toilet paper rolls began circulating on social media and news

outlets, a ripple effect was created. The hidden brain's fear of missing out (FOMO) was activated, pushing more people to stockpile.

• **Amplification of the Scarcity Mindset**: Retailers and media, inadvertently or otherwise, played into the hands of the scarcity mindset. With headlines amplifying the shortage and images of long queues at supermarkets, the perception of scarcity grew exponentially. The hidden brain interpreted these cues as a sign to act quickly.

• **Symbolism of Toilet Paper**: Toilet paper is a staple, representing comfort and hygiene in modern society. The subconscious fear of losing access to such a basic commodity resonated deeply with many, making it a primary target for hoarding.

• **The Domino Effect**: The initial surge in demand led to genuine shortages, which further fueled the panic. This created a feedback loop; as more people witnessed shortages, more felt the urge to hoard, leading to even greater shortages.

• **Cognitive Dissonance**: Once individuals had stockpiled, the hidden brain sought to justify the action, leading to post-purchase rationalization. Many hoarders believed they were right in their actions, citing reasons like the uncertainty of supply chains or the possibility of longer lockdowns.

• **Broader Societal Implications**: The Toilet Paper Scare became a metaphor for the broader panic and response to the pandemic. It highlighted the challenges in information dissemination, the influence of media, and the need for societal solidarity in crisis times.

THE BEANIE BABY CRAZE: A PSYCHOLOGICAL EXPLORATION

The Beanie Baby phenomenon of the 1990s wasn't just a fad; it was a cultural and economic spectacle. These seemingly innocuous stuffed animals took the world by storm, leading to frenzied buying, intense speculation, and even investments. But what lay beneath this craze? Delving deeper, one finds a potent mix of marketing genius, human psychology, and the ever-influential hidden brain.

- **The Illusion of Scarcity**: Ty Inc., the company behind Beanie Babies, masterfully played into the scarcity mindset. They would retire certain models, instantly making them "rare" and highly sought after. The hidden brain, wired to value scarce items more highly, propelled consumers into buying, trading, and collecting fervently.

- **The Collector's Mentality**: Humans have an innate desire to collect and complete sets, a trait stemming from our evolutionary past. Beanie Babies, with their myriad designs and characters, tapped into this desire. Each new release beckoned collectors to obtain it, feeding into a perpetual cycle of acquisition.

- **Social Validation and Herd Behavior**: As Beanie Babies grew in popularity, owning them became a status symbol. The hidden brain's need for social validation and belonging was satiated by jumping onto the Beanie Baby bandwagon. Children wanted them to fit in at school, and adults sought them as conversation starters or even as investments.

- **Emotional Attachment and Anthropomorphism**: The unique designs, names, and little heart-shaped tags with poems made it easy for owners to anthropomorphize and form emotional connections with their Beanie Babies. The hidden brain often associates stuffed animals with comfort, security, and nostalgia from childhood, amplifying the attachment.

- **Media and Hype**: Media played a crucial role in the Beanie Baby mania. Stories of rare Beanie Babies selling for thousands of dollars, coupled with coverage of frenzied consumers lining up at stores, only fueled the fire. The hidden brain interpreted this media attention as validation of the toys' value.

• **Investment and Speculation**: With tales of Beanie Babies being sold for multiples of their purchase price, they began to be seen as investments. The allure of quick profits drove many to buy them in bulk, speculating on future values. This speculative bubble, much like in stock markets, was driven by the hidden brain's optimism bias and the fear of missing out on potential windfalls.

• **The Burst and Aftermath**: As with many speculative bubbles, the Beanie Baby craze eventually burst. As market saturation set in and Ty Inc. continued to release more models, the perceived rarity and value began to wane. The realization that Beanie Babies might not provide the long-term investment returns people had hoped for set in, leading to a rapid decline in demand and value.

JOB SCARCITY: THE PSYCHOLOGY BEHIND EMPLOYMENT ANXIETIES

In contemporary society, job scarcity is a tangible concern for many. Whether real or perceived, the notion that there aren't enough jobs to go around can exert significant psychological, economic, and social pressures on individuals and communities. Beneath the surface of this anxiety lies a complex web of the hidden brain's machinations, societal expectations, and the evolving global economy.

• **Evolutionary Roots of Survival and Security**: At its core, the fear of job scarcity taps into our evolutionary need for survival and security. Stable employment equates to a consistent means of acquiring resources, ensuring our well-being and that of our kin. When the hidden brain perceives a threat to this stability, stress and anxiety responses are triggered.

• **Modern Societal Constructs and Self-worth**: In many cultures, a job is more than just a means of income; it's tied deeply to one's identity and sense of self-worth. The hidden brain associates employment with societal value, respect, and purpose. Job scarcity, therefore, poses a threat not just to financial security but also to personal esteem and societal standing.

- **Media Amplification and Perception**: The role of media in magnifying fears of job scarcity can't be understated. News of layoffs, industries in decline, and economic downturns can exacerbate perceptions of job scarcity. Even if opportunities are available in other sectors or regions, the dominant narrative can influence the collective mindset negatively.

- **The Role of Technology and Globalization**: As automation, AI, and globalization reshape the job landscape, fears of redundancy and job losses are amplified. The hidden brain, resistant to change, can interpret these shifts as direct threats, even if they also present new opportunities in emerging sectors.

- **Competitive Education and Upbringing**: From a young age, many are conditioned to view life as a competition—competing for grades, college admissions, and eventually jobs. This conditioning can reinforce the scarcity mindset, making individuals feel they are constantly vying for limited spots in the job market.

- **Economic Downturns and Reality**: It's important to note that in certain situations, job scarcity is a genuine concern. Economic recessions, industry declines, or significant societal changes can lead to real job losses. In these scenarios, the hidden brain's fears are grounded in reality, making coping mechanisms and adaptive strategies even more vital.

- **Coping Mechanisms and the Rise of Gig Economy**: To counteract job scarcity, many have turned to the gig economy, freelancing, or entrepreneurial ventures. This adaptability showcases the human capacity to find alternative routes to security and purpose when traditional paths are threatened.

- **Collective Psychology and Societal Impact**: On a broader scale, the perception of job scarcity can influence societal morale, consumer confidence, and even political landscapes. When a large segment of the population fears unemployment, it can lead to broader societal shifts and reactions.

. . .

Understanding the roots of job scarcity concerns and differentiating between genuine threats and unfounded fears are crucial in today's ever-evolving job market. By recognizing the role of the hidden brain in these perceptions, individuals can better navigate their career paths, and societies can aim for more holistic solutions to employment concerns.

BREAKING THE CYCLE

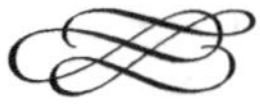

INTRODUCTION TO MINDFULNESS AND MEDITATION

Mindfulness and meditation are powerful tools for disrupting the scarcity mindset. By cultivating a deeper awareness of our thoughts, feelings, and surroundings, we can begin to challenge and reshape the deeply ingrained beliefs and patterns that drive our perception of scarcity.

Mindfulness Practices

Engaging in mindfulness practices can help ground us in the present moment, reducing the anxiety and stress that often accompany the scarcity mindset. Here are some effective mindfulness techniques:

1.Mindful Eating: Engage fully in the experience of eating, savoring each bite, noting textures, flavors, and sensations. This practice helps develop a deeper appreciation for the food we have and the nourishment it provides.

- **How-to**: Take small bites, chew slowly, and focus on the taste, texture, and aroma of your food. Avoid distractions like TV or smartphones while eating.

2.Mindful Walking: Be entirely present with each step, observing the feel of the ground, the rhythm of breathing, and the surrounding environment. This practice fosters a sense of connection to the present moment and the world around us.

- **How-to**: Walk slowly and deliberately, paying attention to the sensations in your feet and legs. Notice the sights, sounds, and smells around you.

3.Active Listening: Fully concentrate, understand, and respond to what others are saying without internal or external distractions. Active listening improves communication and builds stronger, more empathetic relationships.

- **How-to**: Maintain eye contact, nod, and give verbal acknowledgments. Avoid interrupting and reflect back what the speaker has said to ensure understanding.

MEDITATION TECHNIQUES

Meditation can enhance mindfulness by training the mind to maintain focus and cultivate a state of calm. Here are some meditation techniques to practice:

1.Focused Attention Meditation: Concentrate on a single point, often the breath, and continuously bring the mind back whenever it wanders. This practice helps develop concentration and awareness.

- **How-to**: Sit comfortably, close your eyes, and focus on your breath. Count each inhale and exhale up to 10, then start over. If your mind wanders, gently bring your focus back to your breath.

2.Body Scan Meditation: Pay focused attention to various parts of the body, noting sensations, tensions, or emotions. This practice promotes relaxation and body awareness.

- **How-to**: Lie down or sit comfortably. Slowly move your attention through your body, starting from your toes and moving up to your head. Notice any sensations without judgment.

3.Loving-kindness Meditation: Cultivate feelings of compassion and love for oneself and others. This practice can enhance emotional resilience and foster a sense of interconnectedness.

How-to: Sit comfortably, close your eyes, and silently repeat phrases like "May I be happy, may I be healthy, may I be safe." Gradually extend these wishes to others, including loved ones, acquaintances, and even people you find challenging.

CHALLENGES AND MISCONCEPTIONS

Many people encounter challenges and hold misconceptions about mindfulness and meditation. Here are some common ones:

- **"I can't meditate because my mind always wanders."** It's natural for the mind to wander; the practice is about bringing the attention back, strengthening the mental "muscle."
- **"I don't have time to meditate."** Even just a few minutes of focused attention or mindfulness daily can offer significant benefits.

Complementary Practices

Both mindfulness and meditation can be enhanced when paired with complementary practices:

1.Yoga: Physical postures combined with breathwork can help prepare the body and mind for deeper meditation.

- **How-to**: Join a yoga class or follow online tutorials. Focus on the breath and the sensations in your body as you move through different poses.

2.Journaling: Writing can serve as a reflective practice, helping to process and understand experiences from a place of mindfulness.

- **How-to**: Set aside time each day to write about your thoughts, feelings, and experiences. Use prompts like "What am I grateful for today?" or "What challenges did I face and how did I handle them?"

The Power of Awareness

Awareness is the cornerstone of any transformative process. It involves recognizing the subconscious forces at play in our decisions and behaviors. By bringing these hidden elements to light, we can begin to understand their impact and take steps to counteract them.

1.Illuminating the Subconscious: Awareness helps us identify the subconscious patterns and biases that drive our scarcity mindset. By acknowledging these hidden influences, we can begin to address them consciously.

- **How-to**: Practice mindfulness and self-reflection regularly. Pay attention to recurring thoughts and feelings, and explore their origins and impacts.

2.Creating the Space for Choice: With awareness, we gain the power to choose our responses rather than react automatically. This shift from reactive to proactive behavior is crucial in overcoming the scarcity mindset.

- **How-to**: Pause before responding to triggers. Take a few deep breaths and consider different perspectives and options.

3.Empowerment Through Understanding: Understanding the root causes of our behaviors and beliefs gives us the power to change them. Awareness equips us with the knowledge needed to make informed decisions and break free from limiting patterns.

- **How-to**: Seek knowledge and insights through books, workshops, and discussions with others. Reflect on your personal experiences and growth.

PRACTICAL STEPS TO CULTIVATE AWARENESS

1.Mindfulness Practices: Incorporating mindfulness practices such as meditation, deep breathing, or journaling can enhance self-awareness. These practices help us stay present and observe our thoughts and emotions without judgment.

- **How-to**: Dedicate time each day for mindfulness activities. Start with a few minutes and gradually increase the duration as you become more comfortable.

2.Reflective Journaling: Keeping a journal to reflect on daily experiences and emotions can reveal recurring patterns related to scarcity. Regularly reviewing journal entries can provide insights into subconscious beliefs and triggers.

- **How-to**: Write about your thoughts, feelings, and experiences at the end of each day. Use specific prompts to explore your mindset and behaviors.

3.Seeking Feedback: Asking trusted friends, family members, or mentors for feedback can offer an external perspective on our behaviors and mindset. This external input can highlight blind spots we might overlook.

- **How-to**: Regularly seek feedback from others. Be open to their perspectives and use their insights to inform your self-awareness and growth.

4.Professional Help: Working with a therapist or coach can provide structured guidance in uncovering and addressing deep-seated scarcity beliefs. Professional support can facilitate deeper self-exploration and healing.

- **How-to**: Find a qualified therapist or coach who specializes in mindset and personal growth. Schedule regular sessions to work on your awareness and transformation.

STRATEGIES TO OVERCOME THE SCARCITY MINDSET

1.Reframing Negative Thoughts: Practice identifying and reframing negative thoughts related to scarcity. For instance, instead of thinking, "There's never enough time," reframe it to, "I can prioritize what's most important."

- **How-to**: Notice negative thoughts as they arise and consciously choose to reframe them in a positive light. Practice this regularly to develop a habit of positive thinking.

2.Cultivating Gratitude: Regularly practicing gratitude shifts focus from what is lacking to what is abundant. Keeping a gratitude journal or expressing thanks can help reinforce a mindset of abundance.

- **How-to**: Write down three things you're grateful for each day. Share your gratitude with others and reflect on the positive aspects of your life.

3.Setting Realistic Goals: Break down larger goals into smaller, manageable steps. Achieving these smaller milestones can build confidence and reduce the overwhelm associated with scarcity thinking.

- **How-to**: Define your long-term goals and create a step-by-step plan to achieve them. Celebrate each small achievement along the way.

4.Focusing on Abundance: Actively seek and acknowledge examples of abundance in your life. This can include financial stability, supportive relationships, or personal achievements.

- **How-to**: Keep an abundance journal where you note down instances of abundance in your life. Reflect on these regularly to reinforce an abundant mindset.

5.Building a Support Network: Surround yourself with positive influences who encourage growth and abundance. Engaging with a supportive community can provide reinforcement and accountability.

- **How-to**: Join groups or communities that share your values and goals. Build relationships with individuals who inspire and support your growth.

6.Investing in Personal Growth: Continuously invest in your personal development through education, skills training, and self-improvement activities. Building competence and knowledge can reduce feelings of inadequacy and scarcity.

- **How-to**: Enroll in courses, attend workshops, and read books that enhance your knowledge and skills. Commit to lifelong learning and personal growth.

7.Practicing Self-Compassion: Be kind and compassionate towards yourself, especially when confronting ingrained scarcity beliefs. Recognize that change is a gradual process and allow yourself grace.

- **How-to**: Treat yourself with the same kindness and understanding that you would offer a friend. Practice self-compassion exercises and affirmations.

REAL-LIFE EXAMPLES

1.Sarah's Journey to Abundance

- **Background**: Sarah was a marketing executive who constantly felt overwhelmed by her workload and feared she wasn't doing enough to advance her career.
- **Transformation**: She started practicing mindfulness and journaling daily. By becoming more aware of her thoughts and feelings, she identified her scarcity mindset and began to reframe her negative thoughts. Sarah also set realistic goals and celebrated small achievements.
- **Outcome**: Over time, Sarah's anxiety decreased, and she felt more confident in her abilities. She developed a healthier work-life balance and enjoyed her career more.

2.Tom's Path to Financial Stability

- **Background**: Tom struggled with financial insecurity despite having a steady income. He constantly worried about money and avoided spending on anything non-essential.
- **Transformation**: Tom attended a financial literacy course and started working with a financial advisor. He learned to budget, save, and invest wisely. Tom also practiced gratitude and focused on the financial stability he already had.
- **Outcome**: Tom's financial anxiety reduced significantly. He felt more secure and was able to enjoy his money

responsibly. Tom also started investing in his personal growth, taking courses to advance his career.

3.Emma's Creative Awakening

- **Background**: Emma, an aspiring artist, was plagued by self-doubt and the fear that she wasn't talented enough to succeed. This scarcity mindset led to creative blocks and procrastination.
- **Transformation**: Emma joined an artist support group and began practicing mindfulness and positive affirmations. She also set small, achievable creative goals and celebrated each success.
- **Outcome**: Emma's creativity flourished as she overcame her self-doubt. She produced a series of artworks that gained recognition, boosting her confidence and inspiring her to pursue her artistic dreams further.

Breaking free from the scarcity mindset is a journey that begins with awareness and is sustained through conscious effort and practice. By understanding the underlying psychological and subconscious forces, we can implement strategies to foster a mindset of abundance. The path to overcoming scarcity involves continuous self-reflection, mindfulness, and the courage to challenge long-held beliefs. With dedication and support, it is possible to transform the scarcity mindset and embrace a life of abundance and fulfillment.

THE ABUNDANCE MINDSET: AN ANTIDOTE TO SCARCITY

Transitioning from a mindset of scarcity to one of abundance involves more than just changing how we think. It requires a holistic approach that encompasses our actions, environments, and interactions. By fostering a mindset of abundance, we can experience greater fulfillment, creativity, and joy in all aspects of our lives.

Understanding Abundance

Abundance is the belief that there are enough resources, opportunities, and successes for everyone. It contrasts sharply with the scarcity mindset, which focuses on limitations and deficits. Embracing abundance involves recognizing and appreciating the wealth of possibilities around us.

1. **Shifting Perspective**: Cultivating an abundance mindset starts with shifting our perspective. Instead of focusing on what we lack, we focus on what we have and what is possible. This shift can transform how we approach challenges and opportunities.

2. **Gratitude as a Foundation**: Gratitude is a powerful practice that can reinforce an abundance mindset. By regularly acknowledging and appreciating the positive aspects of our lives, we train our minds to see abundance rather than scarcity.

Practical Steps to Foster Abundance

1.Setting Intentional Goals: Define clear, meaningful goals that align with your values and passions. These goals should reflect a belief in your potential and the abundance of opportunities available to you.

- **How-to**: Write down your goals and break them into actionable steps. Regularly review and adjust them as needed.

2.Visualizing Success: Visualization is a technique where you imagine yourself achieving your goals. This practice can enhance motivation, focus, and a sense of possibility.

- **How-to**: Spend a few minutes each day visualizing your goals as already achieved. Picture yourself living your dreams and feeling the emotions associated with your success.

3.Affirmations and Positive Self-Talk: Use affirmations and positive self-talk to reinforce beliefs in abundance and capability. Statements like "I am capable of achieving my goals" or "Opportunities are all around me" can help reshape your mindset.

- **How-to**: Create a list of positive affirmations that resonate with you, such as "I am worthy of abundance" or "Opportunities are all around me." Repeat these affirmations daily, preferably in front of a mirror.

4.Surrounding Yourself with Positivity: The people we interact with can significantly influence our mindset. Surround yourself with positive, supportive individuals who encourage growth and abundance.

- **How-to**: Engage with friends or communities who operate from an abundance mindset. Their perspective and energy can be contagious.

5.Engaging in Acts of Kindness: Acts of kindness, whether big or small, can foster a sense of abundance. When we give to others, we reinforce the belief that there is enough to go around.

- **How-to**: Perform acts of kindness regularly. This could be as simple as complimenting a colleague, helping a neighbor, or donating to a cause you care about.

Continuous Learning and Growth: Commit to lifelong learning and personal development. By constantly seeking to improve and expand your skills, you open yourself to new opportunities and possibilities.

- **How-to**: Enroll in courses, attend workshops, read books, and stay updated on industry trends. Seek opportunities for professional development and personal growth.

The Role of Environment

1.Creating Supportive Spaces: Your physical and digital environments can impact your mindset. Create spaces that inspire and support your goals. This could mean decluttering your home, setting up a dedicated workspace, or curating your social media feeds to include positive content.

- **How-to**: Regularly declutter your living and working spaces. Donate items you no longer need and organize your environment to promote clarity and productivity.

2.Building a Community: Engage with communities that share your values and goals. This could be through local groups, online forums, or professional networks. Being part of a supportive community can reinforce your belief in abundance and provide valuable resources and connections.

- **How-to**: Join professional associations, participate in community events, or start a group focused on shared interests and goals.

CELEBRATING SUCCESSES

1.Recognizing Achievements: Regularly take time to recognize and celebrate your achievements, no matter how small. This practice reinforces a positive feedback loop and encourages continued progress.

- **How-to**: Keep a success journal where you note down your achievements and milestones. Reflect on your progress and celebrate each step forward.

2.Sharing Successes with Others: Sharing your successes can enhance the sense of abundance. Whether through social media, personal interactions, or professional networks, celebrating victories together fosters a collective mindset of abundance.

- **How-to**: Share your achievements with friends, family, or colleagues. Encourage others to share their successes and celebrate together.

3.The Ripple Effect of Sharing: By regularly sharing successes, we foster an environment where achievements are recognized and celebrated. This can boost morale, encourage risk-taking, and inspire others to pursue their dreams.

- **How-to**: Create platforms where team members or community members can share and celebrate their achievements. Actively listen when others share their successes and show genuine interest and joy.

4.Encouraging Others to Share: Actively listen when others share their successes and show genuine interest and joy. Create platforms where team members or community members can share and celebrate their achievements.

- **How-to**: Organize regular team meetings or social gatherings where individuals can share their achievements. Use social media or newsletters to highlight successes within your community.

INTEGRATING ABUNDANCE INTO DAILY LIFE

1.Mindfulness and Meditation

- **Purpose**: Ground yourself in the present and cultivate awareness of abundance.
- **How-to**: Practice mindfulness and meditation daily. Focus on your breath, sensations, and the present moment. This practice helps reduce anxiety and fosters a sense of peace and abundance.

- **Example**: Begin each day with a 10-minute meditation, focusing on your breath and visualizing a day filled with positive experiences.

2.Embracing Change

- **Purpose**: Adapt to new opportunities and challenges with a growth mindset.
- **How-to**: View change as an opportunity for growth rather than a threat. Embrace new experiences, learn from setbacks, and remain open to evolving your path.
- **Example**: When faced with a job change, view it as a chance to grow and develop new skills, rather than focusing on the loss of your previous role.

3.Regular Reflection

- **Purpose**: Continuously assess and realign your mindset and actions.
- **How-to**: Set aside time each week for reflection. Evaluate your progress, celebrate your successes, and identify areas for improvement. This practice ensures you stay aligned with your abundance mindset.
- **Example**: Spend 30 minutes each Sunday reflecting on your achievements and setting intentions for the upcoming week.

ADVANCED TECHNIQUES FOR CULTIVATING ABUNDANCE

1.Energy Management

- **Purpose**: Optimize your physical, emotional, and mental energy to enhance your ability to attract and sustain abundance.

- **How-to**: Practice activities that boost your energy levels, such as regular exercise, adequate sleep, balanced nutrition, and stress management techniques.
- **Example**: Incorporate a daily exercise routine and prioritize sleep to ensure you have the energy needed to pursue your goals.

2.Financial Abundance

- **Purpose**: Develop a healthy financial mindset and habits to attract and manage wealth.
- **How-to**: Educate yourself about personal finance, set financial goals, and practice mindful spending and saving. Invest in assets that appreciate over time and diversify your income streams.
- **Example**: Create a detailed financial plan that includes saving for emergencies, investing for the future, and budgeting for daily expenses.

3.Network Building

- **Purpose**: Build a strong network of supportive relationships that can provide opportunities and resources.
- **How-to**: Attend networking events, join professional organizations, and nurture relationships with mentors and peers. Offer support and value to others in your network.
- **Example**: Schedule regular coffee meetings with colleagues and industry professionals to exchange ideas and build connections.

4.Continuous Learning

- **Purpose**: Embrace lifelong learning to expand your knowledge and skills.

- **How-to**: Enroll in courses, attend workshops, read books, and stay updated on industry trends. Seek opportunities for professional development and personal growth.
- **Example**: Dedicate time each month to read a book related to your field or attend a workshop to learn a new skill.

5.Manifestation Practices

- **Purpose**: Use the power of intention and visualization to attract abundance.
- **How-to**: Practice manifestation techniques such as writing down your goals, visualizing your desired outcomes, and using positive affirmations. Believe in your ability to create the life you desire.
- **Example**: Write down your financial goals for the next year and visualize yourself achieving them with clarity and confidence.

REAL-LIFE EXAMPLES OF ABUNDANCE PRACTICES

1.Corporate Environment

- **Example**: A tech company implements regular mindfulness sessions for employees, encourages them to set personal and professional goals, and celebrates team achievements with monthly recognition events. This creates a supportive and growth-oriented workplace culture.

2.Educational Setting

- **Example**: A university adopts an abundance mindset by offering students opportunities to explore various fields of study, fostering collaboration over competition, and providing resources for personal and academic growth.

Students are encouraged to pursue their passions and share their successes with peers.

3.Community Initiatives

- **Example**: A local community center promotes abundance by organizing skill-sharing workshops, where members teach each other various crafts, trades, and knowledge areas. This fosters a sense of community, mutual support, and continuous learning.

4.Personal Life

- **Example**: An individual practices daily gratitude journaling, sets intentional goals for personal development, and regularly engages in activities that bring joy and fulfillment. They build a network of supportive friends and mentors who encourage their growth.

Cultivating a mindset of abundance is a transformative journey that can profoundly impact every aspect of our lives. By focusing on positivity, continuous growth, and the wealth of opportunities around us, we can break free from the constraints of scarcity. The path to overcoming scarcity involves continuous self-reflection, mindfulness, and the courage to challenge long-held beliefs. With dedication and support, it is possible to transform the scarcity mindset and embrace a life of abundance and fulfillment.

CASE STUDIES

Understanding how the scarcity mindset manifests and can be overcome in real-life scenarios provides practical insights and inspiration. This chapter presents case studies of individuals who grappled with and ultimately transformed their scarcity mindset into one of abundance and fulfillment.

ARJUN – THE ACADEMIC OVERACHIEVER

- **Background**: Arjun had always been the golden boy of his academic circle. From early childhood, he showed a proclivity for studies, always topping his class, winning scholarships, and being the benchmark for academic excellence. However, this reputation came with immense pressure. Every exam, every project was a weight on his shoulders. He wasn't just studying for knowledge; he was studying to maintain his rank, his image, and the expectations that came with it. His days were long, nights longer, and the specter of competition was ever-present.

Even a slight slip in grades led to sleepless nights and anxiety.

- **The Catalyst**: During his second year at university, Arjun attended a seminar on holistic learning and the dangers of competition-driven education. The speaker, a renowned educational psychologist, discussed the virtues of collaborative learning and the deeper understanding that came from passion-driven study as opposed to rank-driven study. One phrase struck Arjun deeply: "Are you studying to prove yourself or improve yourself?"

- **The Shift**: This seminar was a turning point for Arjun. He began questioning his motives behind his relentless pursuit of grades. He realized that in the race to be number one, he had forgotten the joy of learning. He decided to make a change. Instead of isolated study sessions, he initiated group discussions. He reached out to classmates, shared notes, offered to tutor those who struggled, and actively sought help when he found challenging topics.

Arjun started attending workshops, seminars, and conferences related to his field, not for extra credits, but for the sheer joy of learning and networking. He took on projects that he was genuinely passionate about, even if they weren't directly linked to his curriculum.

- **Outcome**: The results of this shift were profound. Arjun's academic performance remained strong, but the anxiety and pressure significantly reduced. He found a renewed passion for his studies, built stronger relationships with his peers, and developed a more holistic understanding of his field. His mental health improved, and he rediscovered the joy of learning for the sake of knowledge.

EMILY – THE CORPORATE CLIMBER

- **Background**: Emily was a rising star in her corporate firm. Ambitious and driven, she quickly climbed the ranks, often putting in long hours and sacrificing personal time for work. She thrived on accolades and promotions, but beneath the surface was a constant fear of not being enough, of losing her edge. This fear manifested in a relentless pursuit of success, often leading to burnout and strained relationships.

- **The Catalyst**: Emily's turning point came during a leadership retreat focused on personal development. One of the exercises involved reflecting on personal values and long-term goals. For the first time, Emily realized how much she had neglected her personal life and well-being in her pursuit of professional success. A coach's words resonated with her: "True success is measured by the quality of your life, not just your career achievements."

- **The Shift**: Determined to make a change, Emily began setting boundaries at work. She prioritized tasks, delegated more, and learned to say no. She also made time for hobbies and activities she loved, such as painting and hiking. Emily started a mindfulness practice, which helped her manage stress and stay present. She sought mentorship and built a support network within and outside her workplace.

- **Outcome**: Emily found a better work-life balance. Her performance at work remained high, but she was no longer driven by fear. She felt more fulfilled and engaged, both professionally and personally. Her relationships improved, and she found joy in activities outside of work. Emily's journey showed her that true abundance comes from a balanced and holistic approach to life.

LIAM – THE FINANCIAL WORRIER

- **Background**: Liam constantly worried about money. Despite having a stable job and a reasonable income, he always felt on the brink of financial disaster. This scarcity mindset led him to save excessively, avoid spending on even necessary items, and constantly stress about future financial security. His fear of financial instability overshadowed his ability to enjoy life.
- **The Catalyst**: A financial literacy workshop at his company opened Liam's eyes to his irrational fears. The speaker emphasized the importance of understanding one's financial situation and planning for the future, but also enjoying the present. A simple exercise of writing down his financial goals and reviewing his actual financial status revealed that he was in a much better position than he thought.
- **The Shift**: Liam decided to take a proactive approach to his finances. He created a realistic budget that included not just savings but also allocations for leisure and personal growth. He invested in a financial advisor who helped him plan for long-term security. Liam also started practicing gratitude, focusing on the financial stability he already had rather than what he feared losing.
- **Outcome**: With a clearer understanding of his finances and a balanced approach to spending and saving, Liam's anxiety decreased. He felt more secure and was able to enjoy his income without guilt. He started traveling, a passion he had long suppressed, and even treated himself to occasional luxuries. Liam's life became richer, both financially and emotionally, as he embraced a mindset of abundance.

MAYA – THE ENTREPRENEURIAL STRUGGLER

- **Background**: Maya ran a small business, and while she was passionate about her work, the constant worry about competition and limited resources plagued her. She often worked long hours, trying to outdo competitors, and frequently felt overwhelmed by the challenges of running a business. Her scarcity mindset made it difficult to see opportunities for growth and collaboration.
- **The Catalyst**: Maya attended a business networking event where a successful entrepreneur shared their journey. The speaker highlighted the importance of collaboration, innovation, and viewing competitors as potential partners rather than threats. This perspective shift was eye-opening for Maya, making her realize she had been limiting her own growth by focusing too much on competition.
- **The Shift**: Inspired by the event, Maya started reaching out to other small business owners. She formed partnerships, shared resources, and even collaborated on projects. She also invested in learning new skills and technologies to innovate her business. By shifting her focus from competition to collaboration, Maya found new ways to grow and improve her business.
- **Outcome**: Maya's business began to thrive. Collaborating with others brought in new ideas, resources, and opportunities that she hadn't considered before. Her stress levels decreased, and she found renewed enthusiasm for her work. Maya's story exemplifies how shifting from a scarcity to an abundance mindset can open doors to growth and success.

Jonathan – The Creative Block

- **Background**: Jonathan was a talented musician who struggled with creative blocks and self-doubt. Despite his skills, he constantly compared himself to other musicians and felt he could never measure up. This scarcity mindset led to procrastination and a lack of new material, hindering his career progress.
- **The Catalyst**: Jonathan attended a creativity workshop that focused on overcoming mental barriers and embracing one's unique artistic voice. The facilitator encouraged participants to let go of comparisons and embrace their individuality. Jonathan realized that his fear of not being as good as others was holding him back.
- **The Shift**: Jonathan began practicing mindfulness and gratitude, focusing on his own growth rather than comparing himself to others. He set small, achievable goals for his music and celebrated each milestone. Jonathan also started collaborating with other artists, which reignited his passion and provided fresh perspectives.
- **Outcome**: Jonathan's creativity flourished as he embraced his unique style and stopped comparing himself to others. He released new music that received positive feedback, and his confidence grew. Jonathan's career took off as he continued to innovate and collaborate, demonstrating the power of an abundance mindset in creative fields.

Sarah – The Overwhelmed Caregiver

- **Background**: Sarah was the primary caregiver for her aging parents. The constant demands of caregiving, combined with her full-time job, left her feeling overwhelmed and drained. Her scarcity mindset made her feel there was never enough time or energy to take care of herself, leading to burnout.
- **The Catalyst**: Sarah attended a support group for caregivers, where she learned about the importance of self-

care and setting boundaries. The facilitator emphasized that taking care of oneself was not selfish but necessary for providing quality care to others.

- **The Shift**: Sarah began implementing small changes in her routine to prioritize self-care. She scheduled regular breaks, asked for help from family members, and engaged in activities that brought her joy. Sarah also practiced mindfulness and gratitude to manage stress and maintain a positive outlook.
- **Outcome**: Sarah's well-being improved significantly as she adopted a more balanced approach to caregiving. She felt more energized and capable of providing better care for her parents. Sarah's journey highlighted the importance of self-care and setting boundaries in maintaining a healthy, abundant life.

These case studies illustrate the profound impact of shifting from a scarcity mindset to one of abundance. Whether in academics, corporate life, personal finances, or entrepreneurship, embracing abundance leads to greater fulfillment, creativity, and success. By learning from these real-life examples, we can find inspiration and practical strategies to transform our own lives.

PRACTICAL EXERCISES AND TECHNIQUES

To effectively transition from a scarcity mindset to an abundance mindset, practical exercises and techniques are essential. These practices help integrate new thought patterns and behaviors into daily life, reinforcing the principles of abundance.

EXERCISES TO CULTIVATE AN ABUNDANCE MINDSET

1.Gratitude Journaling

- **Purpose**: Focus on the positive aspects of your life and reinforce the abundance around you.
- **How-to**: Each day, write down three things you are grateful for. They can be simple or significant. Over time, this practice shifts your focus from what you lack to what you have.
- **Example**: "I am grateful for the supportive conversation I had with my friend today. I am thankful for the delicious meal I enjoyed this evening. I appreciate the peaceful walk I took in the park.

2.Positive Affirmations

- **Purpose**: Rewire your brain to believe in abundance and your ability to attract it.
- **How-to**: Create a list of positive affirmations that resonate with you, such as "I am worthy of abundance" or "Opportunities are all around me." Repeat these affirmations daily, preferably in front of a mirror.
- **Example**: "I attract positive opportunities effortlessly. I am surrounded by abundance in all areas of my life.

3.Visualization

- **Purpose**: Strengthen your belief in your goals and your ability to achieve them.
- **How-to**: Spend a few minutes each day visualizing your goals as already achieved. Picture yourself living your dreams, feeling the emotions associated with your success.
- **Example**: Visualize yourself in your dream job, experiencing the satisfaction and joy of accomplishing your professional goals.

4.Mindful Spending

- **Purpose**: Develop a healthy relationship with money and appreciate the resources you have.
- **How-to**: Before making a purchase, pause and ask yourself if it aligns with your values and goals. Reflect on the joy and utility the purchase will bring you.
- **Example**: Instead of impulsively buying a new gadget, consider whether it enhances your life or fulfills a genuine need.

Acts of Kindness

- **Purpose**: Foster a sense of abundance by giving to others.
- **How-to**: Perform acts of kindness regularly. This could be as simple as complimenting a colleague, helping a neighbor, or donating to a cause you care about.
- **Example**: Volunteer at a local shelter, or surprise a friend with a thoughtful gift or note.

6.Networking and Collaboration

- **Purpose**: Expand your opportunities through connections and shared resources.
- **How-to**: Engage with professional networks, attend industry events, and collaborate with peers. Sharing knowledge and resources can lead to mutually beneficial opportunities.
- **Example**: Join a professional association or attend a networking event to meet like-minded individuals and explore collaborative projects.

Decluttering

- **Purpose**: Clear physical and mental space to make room for abundance.
- **How-to**: Regularly declutter your living and working spaces. Donate items you no longer need and organize your environment to promote clarity and productivity.
- **Example**: Clean out your closet and donate clothes you no longer wear, creating space for new items that bring you joy.

8.Surround Yourself with Abundance Thinkers

- **Purpose**: Create an environment conducive to abundance thinking.
- **How-to**: Engage with friends or communities who operate from an abundance mindset. Their perspective and energy can be contagious.
- **Example**: Join a mastermind group or online community focused on personal growth and abundance.

9.Journaling Successes

- **Purpose**: Recognize and celebrate abundance in your life.
- **How-to**: At the end of each day, jot down a success or a moment where you felt abundant. Over time, this journal will serve as a testament to the abundance in your life.
- **Example**: "Today, I successfully completed a challenging project at work. I felt proud and appreciated for my efforts.

10.Nature Walks

- **Purpose**: Connect with the natural abundance around you.
- **How-to**: Spend time in nature, observing its cycles and endless bounty. Recognize that you, too, are a part of this abundant ecosystem.
- **Example**: Take a walk in a nearby park or forest, noting the diversity and beauty of the plants and wildlife

INTEGRATING ABUNDANCE INTO DAILY LIFE

1.Mindfulness and Meditation

- **Purpose**: Ground yourself in the present and cultivate awareness of abundance.
- **How-to**: Practice mindfulness and meditation daily. Focus on your breath, sensations, and the present moment. This practice helps reduce anxiety and fosters a sense of peace and abundance.
- **Example**: Begin each day with a 10-minute meditation, focusing on your breath and visualizing a day filled with positive experiences.

2.Setting Intentional Goals

- **Purpose**: Align your actions with your values and aspirations.

- **How-to**: Define clear, meaningful goals that reflect your values and passions. Break them down into actionable steps and track your progress regularly.
- **Example**: Set a goal to learn a new skill related to your career, and create a step-by-step plan to achieve it over the next six months.

3.Embracing Change

- **Purpose**: Adapt to new opportunities and challenges with a growth mindset.
- **How-to**: View change as an opportunity for growth rather than a threat. Embrace new experiences, learn from setbacks, and remain open to evolving your path.
- **Example**: When faced with a job change, view it as a chance to grow and develop new skills, rather than focusing on the loss of your previous role.

4.Creating Supportive Environments

- **Purpose**: Foster environments that support your abundance mindset.
- **How-to**: Organize your home and workspace to reflect order and positivity. Surround yourself with reminders of your goals and achievements, such as vision boards or inspirational quotes.
- **Example**: Create a vision board with images and words that represent your goals and place it in a prominent location where you can see it daily.

5.Regular Reflection

- **Purpose**: Continuously assess and realign your mindset and actions.

- **How-to**: Set aside time each week for reflection. Evaluate your progress, celebrate your successes, and identify areas for improvement. This practice ensures you stay aligned with your abundance mindset.
- **Example**: Spend 30 minutes each Sunday reflecting on your achievements and setting intentions for the upcoming week.

ADVANCED TECHNIQUES FOR CULTIVATING ABUNDANCE

1.Energy Management

- **Purpose**: Optimize your physical, emotional, and mental energy to enhance your ability to attract and sustain abundance.
- **How-to**: Practice activities that boost your energy levels, such as regular exercise, adequate sleep, balanced nutrition, and stress management techniques.
- **Example**: Incorporate a daily exercise routine and prioritize sleep to ensure you have the energy needed to pursue your goals.

2.Financial Abundance

- **Purpose**: Develop a healthy financial mindset and habits to attract and manage wealth.
- **How-to**: Educate yourself about personal finance, set financial goals, and practice mindful spending and saving. Invest in assets that appreciate over time and diversify your income streams.
- **Example**: Create a detailed financial plan that includes saving for emergencies, investing for the future, and budgeting for daily expenses.

3.Network Building

- **Purpose**: Build a strong network of supportive relationships that can provide opportunities and resources.
- **How-to**: Attend networking events, join professional organizations, and nurture relationships with mentors and peers. Offer support and value to others in your network.
- **Example**: Schedule regular coffee meetings with colleagues and industry professionals to exchange ideas and build connections.

Continuous Learning

- **Purpose**: Embrace lifelong learning to expand your knowledge and skills.
- **How-to**: Enroll in courses, attend workshops, read books, and stay updated on industry trends. Seek opportunities for professional development and personal growth.
- **Example**: Dedicate time each month to read a book related to your field or attend a workshop to learn a new skill.

5.Manifestation Practices

- **Purpose**: Use the power of intention and visualization to attract abundance.
- **How-to**: Practice manifestation techniques such as writing down your goals, visualizing your desired outcomes, and using positive affirmations. Believe in your ability to create the life you desire.
- **Example**: Write down your financial goals for the next year and visualize yourself achieving them with clarity and confidence.

Integrating these habits into your daily life can create a powerful shift towards an abundance mindset. Over time, these practices can become second nature, guiding you towards a life rich in opportunities, gratitude, and growth. By consciously adopting these exercises and techniques, you can transform your relationship with scarcity and fully embrace the abundance that surrounds you. The journey to an abundance mindset is continuous and requires consistent effort, but the rewards of a fulfilled and prosperous life are well worth it.

SCARCITY MINDSET AND MONEY

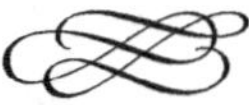

The concept of scarcity is deeply rooted in the fundamental economic problem: unlimited desires clashing with limited resources. When applied to money, scarcity transcends the mere lack of material wealth and delves into the psychological perception of never having enough, regardless of one's financial standing.

THE BASIC ECONOMIC PRINCIPLE

At its core, economics grapples with the allocation of limited resources to meet unlimited needs and wants. In monetary terms, scarcity signifies the gap between available financial resources and the desired financial outcomes. For instance, even if one earns a six-figure salary, they might still feel they don't have enough if their desires or obligations surpass their income.

Perceived vs. Real Scarcity

- **Perceived Scarcity**: Even when resources are available, the perception of scarcity can persist. This often stems from psychological factors, such as fear of future insecurity, comparison with others, or ingrained beliefs about money.
- **Real Scarcity**: Actual financial limitations that restrict one's ability to meet basic needs or achieve desired goals. This can be due to low income, high expenses, debt, or unexpected financial setbacks.

THE ROLE OF MEDIA AND ADVERTISING

Media, especially in its modern digital avatars, plays a pivotal role in shaping consumer behaviors. The continuous barrage of advertisements not only informs but often molds preferences, desires, and notions of 'the good life.'

1. **Creating False Needs**: Advertisements often create a sense of need for products and services that may not be essential, promoting a culture of consumerism.
2. **Promoting Instant Gratification**: The media emphasizes quick fixes and instant gratification, encouraging spending over saving.
3. **Social Comparison**: Social media platforms exacerbate feelings of inadequacy by showcasing curated lifestyles that appear financially abundant.

The Downside of Excessive Consumerism

1. **Financial Strain**: The pressure to 'keep up with the Joneses' can lead to unhealthy financial habits. Over-reliance on credit, leading to debt traps, is a common pitfall for many.
2. **Environmental Concerns**: Fast fashion, tech obsolescence, and the throwaway culture contribute to environmental

degradation. Overconsumption strains natural resources and leads to significant waste.

3. **Mental Health and Well-being**: The relentless pursuit of material possessions can overshadow intrinsic values like relationships, experiences, and personal growth. The constant comparison, often amplified by social media, can lead to dissatisfaction, stress, and other mental health issues.

Finding a Middle Path

1. **Conscious Consumerism**: More and more people are gravitating towards conscious buying, prioritizing quality over quantity, and sustainability over fast consumption.
2. **Minimalism**: A counter-movement to rampant consumerism, minimalism champions the mantra of 'less is more.' It emphasizes the joy in simplicity and the value of possessing only what truly adds value to one's life.
3. **Education and Awareness**: Encouraging financial literacy, environmental education, and mental well-being can help individuals make informed and balanced choices.

Practical Financial Strategies to Overcome Scarcity

1.Budgeting and Planning: Create a realistic budget that aligns with your income and expenses. Planning helps in understanding where your money goes and how to allocate it efficiently.

- **How-to**: Track your income and expenses, categorize them, and identify areas where you can cut back. Use budgeting tools or apps to simplify the process.

2.Emergency Fund: Building an emergency fund provides a financial cushion against unexpected expenses, reducing the anxiety associated with scarcity.

- **How-to**: Aim to save at least three to six months' worth of living expenses. Start small and gradually build your fund by setting aside a portion of your income each month.

3.Investing Wisely: Educate yourself about different investment options and choose those that align with your financial goals and risk tolerance. Investing can help grow your wealth over time.

- **How-to**: Research various investment vehicles such as stocks, bonds, mutual funds, and real estate. Consider consulting a financial advisor to develop a diversified investment portfolio.

4.Debt Management: Develop a plan to manage and reduce debt. Prioritize high-interest debts and consider seeking professional advice if needed.

- **How-to**: List all your debts, prioritize them based on interest rates, and create a repayment plan. Explore debt consolidation options or negotiate with creditors for better terms.

5.Financial Literacy: Continuously educate yourself about personal finance. Understanding how money works and making informed decisions can significantly alleviate the scarcity mindset.

- **How-to**: Read books, attend workshops, and follow reputable financial blogs and podcasts. Stay informed about financial trends and best practices.

6.Mindful Spending: Reflect on your purchases and their alignment with your values and goals. Mindful spending involves making deliberate choices rather than impulsive buys.

- **How-to**: Before making a purchase, ask yourself if it aligns with your long-term goals and values. Consider implementing a "cooling-off" period for major purchases to avoid impulse buying.

Cultivating an Abundance Mindset in Finances

1.Gratitude for Financial Stability: Regularly acknowledge and appreciate your financial stability and the resources you have. Gratitude shifts focus from scarcity to abundance.

- **How-to**: Keep a gratitude journal where you note down financial blessings and achievements. Reflect on how far you've come and the progress you've made.

2.Visualization of Financial Goals: Visualize achieving your financial goals. This practice can enhance motivation and create a positive outlook towards your financial future.

- **How-to**: Create a vision board with images and words that represent your financial goals. Spend a few minutes each day visualizing yourself achieving these goals.

3.Affirmations and Positive Self-talk: Use affirmations to reinforce beliefs in your financial capabilities. Statements like "I am capable of achieving financial success" can help reshape your mindset.

How-to: Write down positive affirmations related to money and repeat them daily. Surround yourself with positive financial influences.

4.Seeking Support and Guidance: Engage with financial advisors, mentors, or support groups to gain insights and advice. Learning from others' experiences can provide valuable perspectives.

How-to: Join financial literacy groups, seek mentorship from financially successful individuals, and attend financial planning seminars.

CASE STUDIES: TRANSFORMING SCARCITY INTO FINANCIAL ABUNDANCE

1.Case Study: Rachel – The Diligent Saver

- **Background**: Rachel was always anxious about money despite having a stable income. She constantly worried about the future and avoided spending even on necessities.
- **The Shift**: Rachel started working with a financial advisor who helped her create a balanced budget and investment plan. She also began practicing gratitude and mindful spending.
- **Outcome**: Rachel's anxiety decreased as she gained confidence in her financial planning. She started enjoying her income and investing in experiences and personal growth, transforming her relationship with money.

2.Case Study: James – The Over-spender

- **Background**: James had a high income but frequently overspent, leading to significant debt. His scarcity mindset drove him to seek validation through material possessions.
- **The Shift**: He attended financial literacy courses and joined a support group for managing debt. James learned to budget, prioritize his spending, and find fulfillment in non-material aspects of life.
- **Outcome**: James paid off his debt and built a substantial emergency fund. He developed healthier spending habits and found satisfaction in financial stability and personal relationships.

3.Case Study: Lily and Mark – The Young Couple

- **Background**: Lily and Mark, newlyweds, struggled with aligning their financial goals and managing their combined finances. They often argued about money, feeling there was never enough.
- **The Shift**: They attended couples' financial counseling and created a joint financial plan. They learned to communicate openly about their financial goals and work together towards them.
- **Outcome**: Lily and Mark developed a strong financial partnership, saving for their future and making informed spending decisions. Their relationship improved as they worked together towards common goals.

4.Case Study: Emily – The Entrepreneur

- **Background**: Emily, a small business owner, faced constant financial uncertainty. Her scarcity mindset led her to make conservative business decisions, limiting her company's growth.
- **The Shift**: She sought mentorship from successful entrepreneurs and invested in financial education for business owners. Emily learned to take calculated risks and leverage resources effectively.
- **Outcome**: Emily's business thrived as she adopted a growth-oriented approach. She expanded her operations, increased her revenue, and developed a resilient mindset towards financial challenges.

The scarcity mindset in relation to money is a complex interplay of economic realities and psychological perceptions. By understanding these dynamics and applying practical financial strategies, we can shift towards a mindset of abundance. This transition involves not just changing how we manage our finances but also how we perceive them. Embracing an abundance mindset leads to healthier financial habits, reduced stress, and a more fulfilling life. The journey to financial abundance requires continuous learning, mindful spending, and the courage to seek help when needed. By fostering a positive relationship with money, we can achieve financial stability and peace of mind.

SCARCITY MINDSET AND RELATIONSHIPS

In the vast realm of human relationships, a scarcity mindset can subtly manifest, shaping how we interact with and perceive our partners, potential partners, and even ourselves. While it might seem counterintuitive in a world abundant with potential connections, especially in the age of social media and online dating, the feeling of scarcity in relationships is very real for many. Recognizing these signs can be the first step toward shifting to a healthier mindset.

SIGNS OF A SCARCITY MINDSET IN RELATIONSHIPS

1.Clinging Behavior and Fear of Being Alone

- **Over-attachment**: Individuals might become overly attached to their partners, wanting to spend every moment with them and feeling restless or anxious when apart.
- **Constant Reassurance**: A constant need for validation and reassurance about the relationship's stability or the partner's feelings.

2.Belief in a Limited Pool of Suitable Partners

- **Settling**: Staying in relationships that aren't fulfilling or even toxic because of the fear that there might not be someone better out there.
- **Rushing**: Hurrying into relationships or pushing them to progress faster than they naturally would due to fear of missing out.

3.Over-compromising on Core Values and Boundaries

- **Compromising Values**: Sacrificing core values and personal boundaries to keep the relationship, often leading to resentment and dissatisfaction.
- **People-Pleasing**: Consistently putting the partner's needs above one's own to avoid conflict or abandonment.

4.Comparison and Jealousy

- **Comparing to Others**: Frequently comparing the relationship or partner to others, often leading to feelings of inadequacy.
- **Jealousy**: Intense jealousy stemming from fear of losing the partner to someone else.

THE IMPACT OF A SCARCITY MINDSET ON RELATIONSHIPS

1. **Emotional Strain**: Constant fear and insecurity can lead to emotional exhaustion for both partners, causing strain in the relationship.
2. **Communication Breakdowns**: Fear of conflict or rejection can hinder open and honest communication, leading to misunderstandings and unresolved issues.

3. **Erosion of Self-esteem**: Continuously compromising personal values and needs can erode self-esteem and self-worth.
4. **Toxic Dynamics**: Settling for unfulfilling relationships can create toxic dynamics, where one or both partners feel trapped and unhappy.

SHIFTING TO AN ABUNDANCE MINDSET

1.Self-awareness and Reflection

- **Recognize Patterns**: Reflect on past relationships to identify recurring patterns of scarcity mindset. Acknowledging these patterns is the first step towards change.
- **Understand Triggers**: Identify triggers that activate the scarcity mindset, such as certain behaviors, situations, or insecurities.

2.Building Self-worth

- **Self-love Practices**: Engage in activities that promote self-love and self-care. This can include hobbies, physical exercise, or meditation.
- **Affirmations**: Use positive affirmations to reinforce self-worth and the belief that you deserve fulfilling relationships.

3.Setting Boundaries

- **Identify Core Values**: Clearly define your core values and what you need in a relationship. Use these as a guide to set healthy boundaries.
- **Communicate Boundaries**: Communicate your boundaries

clearly and respectfully to your partner. Ensure that they are understood and respected.

4.Embracing Authenticity

- **Be True to Yourself**: Embrace your authentic self in relationships. Do not compromise your true self to fit someone else's expectations.
- **Seek Authentic Connections**: Look for relationships where both partners can be their authentic selves and support each other's growth.

5.Practicing Gratitude and Appreciation

- **Gratitude Journals**: Keep a gratitude journal to regularly reflect on and appreciate the positive aspects of your relationship.
- **Express Appreciation**: Regularly express appreciation and gratitude to your partner. Acknowledging and valuing each other strengthens the bond.

6.Expanding Social Circles

- **Meet New People**: Actively seek opportunities to meet new people and expand your social circles. This reduces the fear of limited options.
- **Join Communities**: Participate in communities or groups that align with your interests and values, fostering a sense of belonging and connection.

7.Mindful Communication

- **Active Listening**: Practice active listening, where you fully concentrate on what the other person is saying without interrupting. This fosters understanding and connection.

- **Honest Expression**: Communicate your feelings and needs honestly and openly. Transparency builds trust and intimacy.

CASE STUDIES: OVERCOMING SCARCITY IN RELATIONSHIPS

1.Case Study: Alex and Jamie

- **Background**: Alex and Jamie struggled with constant reassurance and over-attachment in their relationship.
- **The Shift**: They started attending couples therapy, where they learned to communicate their insecurities and build trust.
- **Outcome**: Through consistent effort, they developed a healthier, more secure relationship where both felt valued and understood.

2.Case Study: Sarah

- **Background**: Sarah often rushed into relationships, fearing she would miss out on finding a partner.
- **The Shift**: After a period of self-reflection and personal growth, she began prioritizing her own values and taking time to know her partners better.
- **Outcome**: Sarah eventually found a fulfilling relationship based on mutual respect and shared values.

3.Case Study: Michael

- **Background**: Michael frequently compared his relationships to others, leading to dissatisfaction and jealousy.
- **The Shift**: He started practicing gratitude and focusing on the unique strengths of his relationship.

- **Outcome**: Michael's perspective shifted, allowing him to appreciate and nurture his relationship without constant comparison.

CASE STUDY: EMMA AND TOM

- **Background**: Emma and Tom faced issues with setting and respecting boundaries, leading to frequent conflicts and resentment. Their scarcity mindset made them fear losing each other if they enforced boundaries.
- **The Shift**: They participated in a relationship workshop that emphasized the importance of boundaries and mutual respect. They learned to communicate their needs and respect each other's space.
- **Outcome**: Establishing clear boundaries improved their relationship significantly. They felt more respected and valued, reducing conflicts and increasing their overall satisfaction.

CASE STUDY: LILY

- **Background**: Lily struggled with people-pleasing behaviors, often compromising her values to avoid conflict or rejection. This led to feelings of resentment and loss of identity.
- **The Shift**: Through individual therapy, Lily learned to assert her needs and establish healthy boundaries. She practiced self-affirmation and engaged in activities that reinforced her self-worth.
- **Outcome**: Lily developed a stronger sense of self and began attracting healthier relationships. She felt empowered to be her authentic self and no longer compromised her values.

Transforming a scarcity mindset in relationships into one of abundance requires self-awareness, reflection, and proactive change. By understanding the signs and impacts of scarcity, setting healthy boundaries, and fostering self-worth, individuals can build fulfilling, authentic relationships. Embracing an abundance mindset opens the door to deeper connections, greater happiness, and enduring partnerships.

SCARCITY MINDSET AND PERSONAL GROWTH

The scarcity mindset doesn't just affect our relationships and finances; it can also have a profound impact on our personal growth and creativity. When we operate from a place of scarcity, our potential for growth is stunted, and our creative abilities are hindered. This chapter will explore how a scarcity mindset limits personal development and creativity and provide strategies to foster a growth-oriented and creative mindset.

THE IMPACT OF SCARCITY ON PERSONAL GROWTH

1.Fear of Failure

- **Avoiding Risks**: A scarcity mindset often leads to a fear of failure, which can result in avoiding risks and new opportunities. This fear stems from the belief that failure equates to a lack of ability or worth. Individuals may choose to stay in their comfort zones, missing out on valuable growth experiences.
- **Stagnation**: Without taking risks, personal growth becomes stagnant. Individuals miss out on learning experiences and

the chance to develop new skills. This stagnation can lead to feelings of dissatisfaction and unfulfilled potential.

2.Fixed Mindset

- **Limited Beliefs**: A scarcity mindset is closely related to a fixed mindset, where individuals believe their abilities and intelligence are static and unchangeable. This belief limits their willingness to challenge themselves and pursue growth. They may shy away from opportunities that could foster development.
- **Self-Doubt**: Constant self-doubt and fear of inadequacy prevent individuals from pushing their boundaries and exploring their full potential. This self-doubt can be paralyzing, leading to inaction and missed opportunities.

3.Comparison with Others

- **Measuring Against Others**: The habit of constantly comparing oneself to others can lead to feelings of inadequacy and the belief that there is not enough success to go around. This can diminish motivation and self-esteem, making personal growth seem out of reach.
- **Imposter Syndrome**: Individuals may feel like they don't deserve their achievements, attributing their success to luck rather than their own abilities. This can hinder further growth and development, as they fear being "found out" as frauds.

4.Resource Scarcity

- **Perceived Lack of Time**: Believing that there is not enough time to pursue personal growth can lead to procrastination and inaction. This perception often stems from poor time management or overwhelming commitments.

- **Financial Constraints**: Financial limitations can prevent individuals from investing in their personal growth, such as education, training, or personal development courses. This perceived scarcity can be a significant barrier to growth.

THE IMPACT OF SCARCITY ON CREATIVITY

1.Creative Blocks

- **Fear of Judgement**: The fear of being judged or criticized can paralyze creative expression. Individuals might refrain from sharing their ideas or pursuing creative projects, worried about how others will perceive them.
- **Perfectionism**: A scarcity mindset can lead to perfectionism, where individuals set unrealistically high standards for their creative work. This can result in procrastination and creative blocks, as they fear their work will never be "good enough."

2.Lack of Inspiration

- **Narrow Focus**: When focused on scarcity, individuals often adopt a narrow perspective, limiting their ability to see possibilities and generate new ideas. This narrow focus can stifle creativity and innovation.
- **Burnout**: The constant stress and pressure associated with a scarcity mindset can lead to burnout, depleting the mental energy needed for creative thinking. Burnout can cause a loss of passion and enthusiasm for creative endeavors.

3.Resource Constraints

- **Perceived Lack of Resources**: Individuals may feel that they lack the necessary resources (time, money, skills) to pursue creative endeavors. This belief can prevent them from starting or continuing creative projects, as they focus on what they don't have rather than what they can achieve.

- **Inhibited Experimentation**: Creativity thrives on experimentation and exploration. A scarcity mindset discourages taking risks and trying new approaches, which are essential for creative innovation. Fear of wasting resources can inhibit the willingness to experiment.

4.Self-criticism

- **Harsh Self-judgement**: Individuals with a scarcity mindset often criticize their own work harshly, leading to a lack of confidence in their creative abilities. This self-criticism can stifle creativity and prevent the development of new ideas.
- **Avoidance of Feedback**: Fear of negative feedback can prevent individuals from seeking input from others, missing out on valuable perspectives that could enhance their creative work.

STRATEGIES TO FOSTER A GROWTH-ORIENTED AND CREATIVE MINDSET

1.Embracing a Growth Mindset

- **Belief in Development**: Cultivate the belief that abilities and intelligence can be developed through effort and learning. Embrace challenges as opportunities for growth. This shift in mindset encourages taking on new challenges and learning from them.
- **Learning from Failure**: View failures as learning experiences rather than as reflections of worth. Analyze mistakes to gain insights and improve future efforts. Celebrate the lessons learned from failures as steps towards success.

2.Encouraging Creative Expression

- **Create Without Judgement**: Allow yourself to create without worrying about the end result or the opinions of others. Focus on the process and the joy of creation. This practice reduces the pressure of perfectionism and encourages free expression.
- **Set Realistic Goals**: Break down creative projects into manageable steps. Setting small, achievable goals can reduce the pressure of perfectionism and encourage progress. Celebrate each milestone to build momentum and confidence.

3.Seeking Inspiration

- **Expand Horizons**: Engage in activities that broaden your perspective and inspire creativity, such as reading, traveling, or exploring new hobbies. Exposure to new experiences and ideas fuels creativity.
- **Collaborate**: Collaborate with others to gain new ideas and perspectives. Sharing and discussing creative projects can spark inspiration and innovation. Collaborative efforts often lead to unexpected and innovative outcomes.

4.Overcoming Resource Constraints

- **Utilize Available Resources**: Make the most of the resources you have. Creativity often thrives under constraints, leading to innovative solutions and approaches. Look for ways to repurpose or leverage existing resources.
- **Seek Support**: Don't hesitate to seek support or mentorship. Engaging with communities and networks can provide valuable resources and encouragement. Learning from others' experiences can offer new insights and strategies.

5.Mindfulness and Reflection

- **Practice Mindfulness**: Mindfulness practices can reduce stress and enhance mental clarity, creating a conducive environment for creativity and personal growth. Techniques such as meditation and deep breathing can help maintain focus and calm.
- **Reflect on Progress**: Regularly reflect on your growth and creative journey. Acknowledge achievements and identify areas for improvement without self-criticism. Reflection helps in recognizing patterns and making informed adjustments.

6.Building a Supportive Environment

- **Positive Influences**: Surround yourself with people who encourage and support your growth and creativity. Positive influences can provide motivation and constructive feedback.
- **Creative Spaces**: Create physical and mental spaces that inspire creativity. A dedicated workspace free of distractions can significantly enhance creative output.

7.Continuous Learning

- **Invest in Education**: Continuously seek opportunities for learning and self-improvement. Courses, workshops, and seminars can provide new skills and knowledge that fuel personal and creative growth.
- **Stay Curious**: Cultivate a sense of curiosity and wonder. Ask questions, explore new topics, and remain open to new ideas. Curiosity drives innovation and personal development.

8.Balancing Work and Rest

- **Avoid Burnout**: Ensure a balance between work and rest to maintain mental and physical health. Overworking can lead to burnout, which stifles creativity and growth.
- **Rest and Recharge**: Take regular breaks to rest and recharge. Activities such as nature walks, hobbies, and relaxation techniques can rejuvenate the mind and body.

CASE STUDIES: TRANSFORMING SCARCITY INTO GROWTH AND CREATIVITY

1.Case Study: Emma – The Aspiring Writer

- **Background**: Emma, an aspiring writer, struggled with perfectionism and fear of judgment, leading to severe writer's block.
- **The Shift**: She joined a writing group where members shared their work and provided constructive feedback. This supportive environment helped her overcome her fears. Emma also practiced daily writing exercises without worrying about the outcome.
- **Outcome**: Emma started writing regularly and published her first short story. She continued to grow as a writer, embracing challenges and learning from feedback. Her confidence in her writing abilities grew, and she found joy in the creative process.

2.Case Study: Mark – The Reluctant Entrepreneur

- **Background**: Mark had a great business idea but was paralyzed by the fear of failure and the belief that he lacked the resources to start his business.
- **The Shift**: He attended entrepreneurship workshops and sought mentorship from experienced business owners. These resources helped him build confidence and a growth-

oriented approach. Mark also developed a detailed business plan to manage his resources effectively.

- **Outcome**: Mark successfully launched his business and continued to innovate. He viewed setbacks as learning opportunities and steadily grew his venture. His business thrived as he applied creative solutions to overcome challenges.

3.Case Study: Sophia – The Blocked Artist

- **Background**: Sophia, a talented artist, experienced creative blocks due to self-doubt and fear of criticism.
- **The Shift**: She started practicing mindfulness and set small, achievable art goals. She also began sharing her work in supportive online communities. Sophia experimented with different art styles and mediums, allowing herself to explore without fear of judgment.
- **Outcome**: Sophia's creativity flourished as she embraced a growth mindset. She experimented with new techniques and mediums, gaining confidence and recognition in the art community. Her artwork gained popularity, and she found fulfillment in her creative journey.

4.Case Study: Rachel – The Burned-out Professional

- **Background**: Rachel, a marketing professional, experienced burnout from constantly overworking and striving for perfection.
- **The Shift**: She started practicing mindfulness and implemented a better work-life balance. Rachel also sought professional development courses to enhance her skills and stay inspired.
- **Outcome**: Rachel's productivity and creativity improved as she learned to manage stress and prioritize her well-being.

She developed innovative marketing strategies that gained recognition within her company, leading to a promotion.

5.Case Study: Tom – The Skeptical Scientist

- **Background**: Tom, a scientist, struggled with a fixed mindset, believing that his intelligence and abilities were static.
- **The Shift**: He started attending seminars on growth mindset and engaged in continuous learning through online courses and workshops. Tom began collaborating with colleagues on research projects, sharing ideas and insights.
- **Outcome**: Tom's research productivity increased, leading to significant breakthroughs. He became more open to new ideas and methodologies, enhancing his scientific contributions. His collaborative efforts resulted in published papers and recognition in his field.

The scarcity mindset can significantly hinder personal growth and creativity. By recognizing its impact and adopting strategies to foster a growth-oriented and creative mindset, individuals can unlock their full potential. Embracing challenges, seeking inspiration, and overcoming resource constraints are key steps towards achieving personal development and creative fulfillment. Transforming scarcity into abundance is a journey that requires continuous effort and reflection, but the rewards of growth and creativity are invaluable.

BUILDING RESILIENCE TO MAINTAIN AN ABUNDANCE MINDSET

Building and maintaining an abundance mindset is an ongoing journey that requires resilience, adaptability, and continuous growth. Resilience enables individuals to bounce back from setbacks, overcome challenges, and sustain a positive outlook even in the face of adversity. This chapter explores the concept of resilience, its relationship with the abundance mindset, and practical strategies to cultivate and strengthen resilience in daily life.

UNDERSTANDING RESILIENCE

Resilience is the ability to adapt positively to stress, adversity, or trauma. It involves a combination of mental, emotional, and behavioral flexibility that allows individuals to navigate life's challenges while maintaining their well-being.

1.**Characteristics of Resilient Individuals**:

- **Adaptability**: The ability to adjust to new circumstances and recover from disruptions.
- **Optimism**: Maintaining a positive outlook and finding hope even in difficult situations.

- **Emotional Regulation**: Managing and expressing emotions effectively to prevent overwhelm.
- **Problem-Solving Skills**: The capacity to identify solutions and take proactive steps to address issues.

2.The Role of Resilience in an Abundance Mindset:

- Resilience supports the maintenance of an abundance mindset by helping individuals stay focused on opportunities and growth, rather than being derailed by setbacks and limitations.
- A resilient person is more likely to view challenges as temporary and surmountable, reinforcing the belief in the availability of resources and possibilities.

BUILDING RESILIENCE: PRACTICAL STRATEGIES

1.Developing a Growth Mindset

- **Purpose**: Embrace the belief that abilities and intelligence can be developed through effort and learning.
- **How-to**: Challenge fixed beliefs about your capabilities and focus on learning from experiences. Celebrate progress and view failures as opportunities for growth.
- **Example**: When faced with a challenging project at work, approach it as a chance to develop new skills rather than fearing potential failure.

2.Strengthening Social Connections

- **Purpose**: Build a support network of family, friends, and colleagues who provide emotional support and practical assistance.
- **How-to**: Foster strong, positive relationships by investing time and energy in meaningful interactions.

Seek out communities that share your values and interests.

- **Example**: Join a local club or online group focused on a hobby or cause you are passionate about, and actively participate in discussions and activities.

3.Practicing Self-Compassion

- **Purpose**: Treat yourself with kindness and understanding, especially during times of stress or failure.
- **How-to**: Recognize that everyone experiences setbacks and challenges. Avoid self-criticism and instead offer yourself encouragement and support.
- **Example**: After making a mistake, instead of berating yourself, acknowledge the difficulty of the situation and remind yourself of past successes.

4.Enhancing Emotional Regulation

- **Purpose**: Improve your ability to manage and respond to emotions in a healthy way.
- **How-to**: Practice mindfulness, deep breathing exercises, and journaling to process and understand your emotions. Seek professional help if needed.
- **Example**: When feeling overwhelmed, take a few minutes to practice deep breathing and write down your thoughts to gain clarity and calm.

5.Building Problem-Solving Skills

- **Purpose**: Increase your capacity to identify, analyze, and solve problems effectively.
- **How-to**: Break down problems into smaller, manageable parts. Use brainstorming and critical thinking techniques to explore solutions.

- **Example**: Faced with a complex issue at work, list out the specific challenges, brainstorm potential solutions, and create a step-by-step action plan.

6.Maintaining Physical Health

- **Purpose**: Support overall well-being by taking care of your body through regular exercise, proper nutrition, and adequate sleep.
- **How-to**: Establish a balanced routine that includes physical activity, healthy eating habits, and sufficient rest.
- **Example**: Incorporate a daily exercise routine, such as a morning jog or yoga session, and prioritize a balanced diet and sleep schedule.

7.Cultivating Optimism

- **Purpose**: Develop a habit of looking for the positive aspects of situations and expecting good outcomes.
- **How-to**: Practice gratitude, reframe negative thoughts, and focus on strengths and opportunities.
- **Example**: Start a daily gratitude journal where you list three things you are grateful for each day, and make a conscious effort to see challenges as chances for growth.

CASE STUDIES: RESILIENCE IN ACTION

1.Case Study: Lisa – The Small Business Owner

- **Background**: Lisa, a small business owner, faced significant challenges during an economic downturn. Her sales plummeted, and she struggled to keep her business afloat.
- **Resilience Strategies**: Lisa adopted a growth mindset, sought support from her network, and focused on problem-

solving. She diversified her product line and utilized online marketing to reach new customers.

- **Outcome**: Lisa's resilience allowed her to navigate the downturn successfully. Her business not only survived but thrived, demonstrating the power of adaptability and perseverance.

2.Case Study: David – The Athlete

- **Background**: David, a professional athlete, suffered a severe injury that threatened to end his career. He faced physical and emotional challenges during his recovery.
- **Resilience Strategies**: David practiced self-compassion, focused on physical rehabilitation, and maintained an optimistic outlook. He also leaned on his support network for encouragement.
- **Outcome**: David made a remarkable recovery and returned to his sport. His resilience helped him overcome adversity and achieve new levels of performance.

3.Case Study: Maria – The Academic

- **Background**: Maria, a Ph.D. student, experienced a major setback when her research was criticized and funding was cut. She felt overwhelmed and considered quitting.
- **Resilience Strategies**: Maria sought feedback, embraced a growth mindset, and improved her problem-solving skills. She also connected with mentors for guidance and support.
- **Outcome**: Maria revised her research approach and secured new funding. Her resilience enabled her to complete her Ph.D. successfully and advance her academic career.

CREATING A RESILIENT ENVIRONMENT

1.Fostering a Positive Workplace Culture

- **Purpose**: Create a supportive and growth-oriented workplace that encourages resilience among employees.
- **How-to**: Promote open communication, provide opportunities for professional development, and recognize achievements. Encourage work-life balance and offer support during challenging times.
- **Example**: Implement regular team-building activities and provide access to mental health resources and training programs.

2.Supporting Resilient Families

- **Purpose**: Build a resilient family environment where members support each other and navigate challenges together.
- **How-to**: Encourage open dialogue, practice empathy, and establish family routines that promote well-being. Foster a sense of unity and shared responsibility.
- **Example**: Hold regular family meetings to discuss issues and celebrate successes. Create family traditions that strengthen bonds and provide stability.

3.Strengthening Community Resilience

- **Purpose**: Develop a resilient community that can collectively address and overcome challenges.
- **How-to**: Build strong social networks, promote inclusivity, and encourage community engagement. Develop emergency preparedness plans and support local initiatives.
- **Example**: Organize community events and volunteer

opportunities that bring people together. Establish support groups and resources for vulnerable populations.

Resilience is a vital component of maintaining an abundance mindset. By cultivating resilience through practical strategies and fostering supportive environments, individuals can navigate life's challenges with confidence and optimism. Building resilience is an ongoing process that enhances well-being and sustains a positive outlook, enabling us to thrive in both good times and bad.

THE FUTURE OF ABUNDANCE

As we move further into the 21st century, the concept of abundance is evolving. Technology, global connectivity, and shifting societal values are transforming how we perceive and experience abundance. This final chapter explores the future of abundance, examining emerging trends, innovations, and cultural shifts that are reshaping our understanding of what it means to live abundantly.

TECHNOLOGICAL ADVANCEMENTS AND ABUNDANCE

Technology is a significant driver of abundance in the modern world, offering unprecedented access to resources, information, and opportunities. The following areas highlight how technology is fostering a future of abundance:

1.**Digital Connectivity**

- **Global Access**: The internet has connected billions of people worldwide, enabling access to information, education, and communication like never before.

- **Virtual Collaboration**: Remote work and digital collaboration tools are breaking down geographical barriers, allowing individuals to work together from anywhere in the world.
- **Example**: Online education platforms provide learning opportunities to people in remote areas, enhancing their knowledge and skills without the need for physical presence.

2.Artificial Intelligence and Automation

- **Efficiency and Productivity**: AI and automation are transforming industries by improving efficiency and productivity, reducing the need for repetitive manual labor.
- **Innovative Solutions**: AI is driving innovations in healthcare, agriculture, and various other fields, creating solutions that were previously unimaginable.
- **Example**: AI-powered medical diagnostics can analyze vast amounts of data quickly, leading to earlier detection and treatment of diseases.

3.Renewable Energy

- **Sustainable Resources**: Advances in renewable energy technologies, such as solar and wind power, are making sustainable energy more accessible and affordable.
- **Environmental Impact**: Transitioning to renewable energy reduces dependence on fossil fuels and mitigates environmental damage, promoting long-term abundance.
- **Example**: Solar panels installed in rural communities provide reliable and clean energy, improving the quality of life and economic opportunities.

CULTURAL SHIFTS AND ABUNDANCE

Cultural shifts are also playing a crucial role in shaping the future of abundance. As societies evolve, new values and priorities emerge, influencing how we perceive and pursue abundance.

1.Minimalism and Sustainability

- **Quality Over Quantity**: Minimalism emphasizes owning fewer, higher-quality items, reducing clutter and promoting a sense of abundance through simplicity.
- **Environmental Consciousness**: Sustainable living practices prioritize the health of the planet, recognizing that true abundance includes a healthy environment.
- **Example**: Eco-friendly products and sustainable lifestyle choices are becoming mainstream, reflecting a shift towards more mindful consumption.

2.Holistic Well-being

- **Physical, Mental, and Emotional Health**: Holistic well-being considers all aspects of health, emphasizing balance and harmony in life.
- **Work-Life Integration**: The focus on work-life integration, rather than mere balance, recognizes the need for flexibility and fulfillment in both professional and personal spheres.
- **Example**: Wellness programs in workplaces promote physical activity, mental health support, and personal growth opportunities for employees.

3.Community and Shared Resources

- **Collaborative Consumption**: The sharing economy encourages the use of shared resources, reducing waste and fostering a sense of community.

- **Social Support Networks**: Strong social support networks enhance individual resilience and create a collective sense of abundance.
- **Example**: Community gardens and co-housing projects exemplify how shared resources and communal living can enhance well-being and sustainability.

INNOVATIONS IN ABUNDANCE

Innovative approaches and technologies are continuously emerging, offering new ways to cultivate and experience abundance. Here are some groundbreaking innovations poised to shape the future:

1.Blockchain and Decentralization

- **Transparent Transactions**: Blockchain technology ensures transparency and security in transactions, fostering trust and reducing fraud.
- **Decentralized Finance**: Decentralized finance (DeFi) platforms provide financial services without traditional intermediaries, increasing access to banking and investment opportunities.
- **Example**: Blockchain-based supply chains enhance traceability and accountability, ensuring fair trade and reducing inefficiencies.

2.Circular Economy

- **Resource Efficiency**: The circular economy model focuses on designing out waste and keeping products and materials in use for as long as possible.
- **Economic Resilience**: By promoting reuse, recycling, and regeneration, the circular economy enhances economic resilience and sustainability.
- **Example**: Companies that refurbish and resell electronics

contribute to a circular economy, reducing electronic waste and conserving resources.

3.Regenerative Agriculture

- **Soil Health and Biodiversity**: Regenerative agriculture practices restore soil health, increase biodiversity, and enhance ecosystem services.
- **Food Security**: By improving soil fertility and resilience, regenerative agriculture contributes to long-term food security and sustainable farming.
- **Example**: Farms that use cover cropping, crop rotation, and reduced tillage practices improve soil structure and productivity, supporting sustainable agriculture.

EMBRACING ABUNDANCE IN THE DIGITAL AGE

The digital age offers unique opportunities and challenges for cultivating an abundance mindset. Here are strategies for embracing abundance in an increasingly digital world:

1.Digital Literacy and Empowerment

- **Skill Development**: Continuous learning and skill development are crucial for thriving in the digital age. Embrace digital literacy to leverage technology effectively.
- **Empowerment Through Access**: Ensure equitable access to digital tools and resources, empowering individuals and communities to participate fully in the digital economy.
- **Example**: Initiatives that provide coding and technology training to underserved populations promote digital inclusion and economic empowerment.

2.Mindful Technology Use

- **Balanced Engagement**: Use technology mindfully to enhance well-being and productivity, avoiding over-reliance and digital fatigue.
- **Digital Detox**: Periodically disconnect from digital devices to recharge and reconnect with the physical world and personal relationships.
- **Example**: Implement regular digital detox periods, such as tech-free weekends, to foster balance and reduce stress.

3.Virtual and Augmented Reality

- **Enhanced Experiences**: Virtual and augmented reality technologies offer immersive experiences that can enhance learning, creativity, and social interaction.
- **New Opportunities**: These technologies create new opportunities for remote collaboration, entertainment, and therapeutic applications.
- **Example**: Virtual reality training programs provide immersive learning experiences for students and professionals, enhancing skill acquisition and engagement.

THE FUTURE OF WORK AND ABUNDANCE

The future of work is rapidly evolving, influenced by technological advancements, changing societal expectations, and global trends. Embracing abundance in the workplace involves reimagining work environments, roles, and practices.

1.Flexible Work Arrangements

- **Remote and Hybrid Work**: Flexible work arrangements offer employees greater autonomy and work-life integration, contributing to higher job satisfaction and productivity.
- **Outcome-Based Performance**: Shift from time-based to

outcome-based performance evaluations, focusing on results rather than hours worked.

- **Example**: Companies that implement flexible work policies and prioritize employee well-being report higher levels of engagement and retention.

2.Lifelong Learning and Adaptability

- **Continuous Education**: Encourage lifelong learning and professional development to keep pace with rapidly changing industries and technologies.
- **Adaptive Skills**: Cultivate adaptive skills such as creativity, critical thinking, and emotional intelligence to navigate complex and dynamic work environments.
- **Example**: Organizations that offer ongoing training and development opportunities help employees stay competitive and motivated.

3.Inclusive and Diverse Workplaces

- **Equity and Inclusion**: Foster inclusive and diverse workplaces where all employees feel valued and supported, driving innovation and collaboration.
- **Diverse Perspectives**: Leverage diverse perspectives to solve problems creatively and address a broader range of market needs.
- **Example**: Inclusive hiring practices and diversity training programs create a more equitable and dynamic work environment.

The future of abundance is shaped by our collective actions and choices. By embracing technological advancements, cultural shifts, and innovative approaches, we can create a world where abundance is accessible to all. Building resilience, fostering community, and promoting sustainability are key to maintaining an abundance mindset in the face of evolving challenges. As we look to the future, let us commit to nurturing a mindset of abundance, ensuring that the opportunities and resources of tomorrow are available for everyone.

CONCLUSION: JOURNEYING FROM SCARCITY TO ABUNDANCE

REFLECTING ON THE JOURNEY

As we come to the end of this book, it's essential to reflect on the journey we've undertaken together—from understanding the intricacies of the scarcity mindset to exploring practical strategies for cultivating an abundance mindset. This journey is not just about shifting our thoughts but transforming our entire approach to life, enabling us to embrace opportunities, foster growth, and enrich our personal and collective well-being.

Key Takeaways

1. **Understanding the Hidden Brain**: We delved into the hidden brain's role in perpetuating the scarcity mindset, revealing how subconscious processes influence our thoughts and behaviors. By bringing these processes to light, we can start to challenge and change them.
2. **Practical Strategies**: Throughout the chapters, we explored various techniques to overcome the scarcity mindset, such as mindfulness, gratitude, setting realistic goals, and

building resilience. These strategies are practical tools to help us navigate life's challenges with a positive outlook.

3. **Real-life Applications**: We examined numerous real-life examples and case studies demonstrating how individuals from different walks of life have successfully transitioned from a scarcity mindset to one of abundance. These stories serve as inspiration and proof that change is possible.

4. **Cultivating Resilience**: Building resilience emerged as a crucial factor in maintaining an abundance mindset. By developing emotional regulation, fostering social connections, and practicing self-compassion, we can strengthen our ability to adapt and thrive.

5. **Future of Abundance**: We looked ahead to the future, considering how technological advancements, cultural shifts, and innovative practices can shape a world of abundance. Embracing these changes with a forward-thinking mindset is key to ensuring a prosperous future.

THE PATH FORWARD

Transitioning from a scarcity mindset to one of abundance is a continuous process. It requires dedication, self-reflection, and a commitment to personal growth. Here are some steps to continue on this path:

- **Continuous Learning**: Stay curious and open to new knowledge and experiences. Lifelong learning is essential for personal development and adapting to changing circumstances.
- **Mindful Practice**: Incorporate mindfulness practices into your daily routine. Whether through meditation, journaling, or simply taking a moment to breathe, mindfulness helps maintain focus and clarity.
- **Community Engagement**: Surround yourself with supportive and positive individuals. Engage with

communities that uplift and inspire you, fostering a collective sense of abundance.

- **Setting Intentions**: Regularly set and review your intentions and goals. Keep them aligned with your values and passions, and celebrate your progress along the way.
- **Embracing Change**: Be open to change and view challenges as opportunities for growth. Flexibility and adaptability are crucial for navigating the complexities of life.

Final Thoughts

The journey from scarcity to abundance is deeply personal, yet universally applicable. It's about recognizing the richness of life, even in its simplest forms, and understanding that true wealth goes beyond material possessions. It's about fostering connections, embracing growth, and finding joy in the journey itself.

As you move forward, remember that abundance is not a destination but a way of being. It's a mindset that empowers you to see possibilities where others see limitations, to give generously, and to live fully. Embrace this journey with an open heart and mind, and watch as your world transforms in ways you never thought possible.

Thank you for embarking on this journey. May your path be filled with abundance, joy, and endless possibilities.

ACKNOWLEDGMENTS

I am deeply grateful to everyone who supported me in the creation of this book, "Scarcity Mindset Hidden Brain: Unveiling the Subconscious Forces that Shape Our Choices." This journey would not have been possible without the encouragement, guidance, and love from many incredible individuals.

First and foremost, I would like to thank my family. Your unwavering support, patience, and understanding have been my anchor throughout this process. To my spouse, Olga Brandon, thank you for being my rock, providing me with the strength and inspiration I needed to complete this work. To my children, Mark J., your curiosity and boundless energy remind me daily of the importance of growth and learning.

A special thank you to my mentors and colleagues in the field of psychology. Your insights, feedback, and encouragement have been invaluable. I am particularly grateful to Rodolf Minguer, whose expertise and mentorship have profoundly influenced my work.

To my friends and early readers, thank you for your honest feedback and encouragement. Your perspectives have enriched this book and helped me see my work through different lenses.

Finally, I want to extend my gratitude to you, the reader. Your interest in exploring the depths of the human mind and your commitment to personal growth are what make this journey worthwhile. I hope this book provides you with valuable insights and practical tools to cultivate an abundance mindset and live a more fulfilling life.

Request for Reviews

If you found "Scarcity Mindset Hidden Brain: Unveiling the Subconscious Forces that Shape Our Choices" valuable and insightful, I would greatly appreciate it if you could take a moment to leave a review on Amazon. Your feedback not only helps me improve my work but also assists other readers in discovering this book. Reviews are an essential part of reaching a broader audience and spreading the message of abundance and personal growth.

Thank you for your support, and I look forward to hearing your thoughts and reflections on the book.

With gratitude,

Mark R. William

ABOUT THE AUTHOR

From Scarcity to Abundance: My Personal Journey

To understand the passion and determination behind the pages of this book, I believe it's essential for me to share a piece of my own story.

The heart of winter, 1995. The pangs of hunger were nothing new to me. Wrapped in layers of hand-me-down clothes, I'd trudge through snow-laden streets of New York, clutching a stack of resumes, hoping for a chance. Every "no" from potential employers seemed to echo the same sentiment I'd been hearing my entire life – I was not enough, and I did not have enough.

The scarcity mindset wasn't something I'd read about in books back then; I lived it. Every day was a testament to the crippling fear that tomorrow wouldn't be better, that this was the best life had to offer. My childhood was marked by evictions, the constant jingle of coins to make ends meet, and a silently resilient mother who worked three jobs.

One particular evening, after another day of fruitless job searching, I found myself in a city library. To keep warm, I picked up a book on the philosophy of abundance. It spoke of a mindset where the universe wasn't a place of lack but of infinite possibilities. It suggested that our realities are shaped more by our internal compass than external circumstances.

Skepticism was my first reaction. How could mere thoughts counteract the tangible reality of my empty pockets? But a voice within nudged me to try. What did I have to lose?

I began with small steps. Mindfulness became a haven – those few minutes where the world's chaos dimmed, and I tuned into my abundant spirit. I started to journal, not of my struggles but of my victories, no matter how minuscule. The more I focused on abundance, the more it seemed to manifest. I landed a modest job, which didn't pay much but gave me a platform. From there, every opportunity became a stepping stone, not just to get more but to be more, to give more.

Fast forward to today, I've been blessed with a journey filled with ups and downs, failures, and triumphs. From a struggling young man in a city that never sleeps to an entrepreneur, mentor, and now, an author. My life became a testimony to the principles I'd once scoffed at.

Why did I write this book? Not just to share research and insights on the scarcity vs. abundance mindset but to tell anyone out there still trapped in the claws of scarcity: I've been there. And if I could find a way out, so can you.

To those reading this, my story isn't unique. It's a testament to the human spirit and its ability to transcend. Our minds are powerful tools. In them lie the seeds of scarcity or the blossoms of abundance. The choice of which garden to nurture rests with us.

Thank you for letting me share my journey with you. Through these pages, I hope to be a part of yours. Remember, abundance isn't just about what you have; it's about who you become in the process.

www.ingramcontent.com/pod-product-compliance
Lightning Source LLC
Chambersburg PA
CBHW071214260726
48653CB00041B/492